THE WAY
THE
TRUTH
THE LIFE
John 14:6

Written by Rory Bracken

Testify World Ministries

The Way The Truth The Life

Copyright © 2024 by Rory Bracken. All rights reserved.

No part of this publication may be reproduced, stored in a retrieval system or transmitted in any way by any means, electronic, mechanical, photocopy, recording or otherwise without the prior permission of the author except as provided by USA copyright law.

The opinions expressed by the author are not necessarily those of URLink Print and Media.

1603 Capitol Ave., Suite 310 Cheyenne, Wyoming USA 82001
1-888-980-6523 | admin@urlinkpublishing.com

URLink Print and Media is committed to excellence in the publishing industry.

Book design copyright © 2024 by URLink Print and Media. All rights reserved.

Published in the United States of America

Library of Congress Control Number: 2024924736
ISBN 978-1-68486-991-6 (Paperback)
ISBN 978-1-68486-998-5 (Digital)

18.11.24

THE WAY
—THE—
TRUTH
THE LIFE

Contents

The Body and the Church 1

Faith 5

What Baptism do we need for salvation? 77

Jesus Christ, Servant of God 113

The Key to Salvation: Virtue = First Fruits of Christ 136

Jesus Walk On Water 173

David and GOLIATH 175

Woman at the Well 178

Jonah and the Whale 181

Parable of Prodigal Son 184

Mysteries of the LORD Revealed 192

Prophetic Word 214

Conclusion 229

The Body and the Church

The Name of Jesus has become a lucrative money generating business.

Salvation is now "sold" to those who can afford to fund the leaders of small- or mega churches/ministries through high tithing and thus keep them in the prosperous way they have claimed for themselves as being representatives of Jesus Christ or ministers of His gospel.

Churches are built to accommodate the multitudes that seek the Lord but to no avail. The Lord is not present in the churches who are preaching false doctrine and the faith of the congregations is in vain.

The perception is that the bigger and more prosperous the church, the bigger the Lord's presence and blessings, so it is then concluded that the Lord's approval must rest upon these ministries and all associated with it. The Lord's blessings are spiritual and not connected to accumulation of wealth, health and prosperity by the things of the world. His blessings are given to those who grow in faith and increase in virtue that is equal to Him.

The Lord's people are being misled and are dying for a lack of knowledge pertaining to the true Gospel of Salvation. The focus of many ministries are not on the flock, but on enriching themselves through preaching that which is most common to man, his lust for the things of this world and the fallen nature for which he is constantly condemned by the defiled conscience, that accuses the weak will for its lack of strength to overcome sin.Church leaders are now preaching from the podium they have appointed themselves to, a form of psychology and not the gospel of salvation.

The Body of Christ is the Church of Jesus Christ. They are those who repented and confessed Jesus Christ as the Saviour and redeemer of all mankind, being the Son of God and baptized with the Holy Spirit, joined to God in His Spiritual covenant.

The true Body of Christ is in unity of the Spirit and functions as a whole being united in one truth, one Spirit and in one mind, in an environment fruitful for faith, serving God in Spirit and truth, by abiding in Him and observing Him in all things holy and sanctified by His Blood.

A Building of bricks and cement, is not the House of the Lord, for the Temple of the Lord is within those in whom His Spirit abides in.

The Glory of the Lord is His virtue that is born within each one that is of the Spirit joined to Him.

In the tabernacle of Moses, the glory of the Lord visited the inner sanctuary and so He manifested His presence to His chosen nation, but that has passed and Jesus established a Spiritual Covenant, through which the body of a believer is now the temple of the Lord.

1 Cor 6:19

"What? Know ye not that the body is the temple of the Holy Ghost which is in you, which ye have of God, and ye are not your own?" This is He who comes by water and blood-Jesus Christ; only by water, but by water and blood. and it is the Spirit who bears witness, because the Spirit truth. For there are three that bare witness in heaven: the Father, the Word, and the Holy Spirit; and these three are one. and there are three that bear witness on earth: the Spirit, the Water, and the Blood, and these three

agree as one. if we receive the witness of men,the witness of God is greater; for this is the witness of God which he has testified of His Son. He who believes in the son of God has the witness in himself; He who does not believe God has made him a liar, because he has not believed the testimony that God has given of his son. And this is the testimony: that God has given us eternal life, and this life is in his son. He who has the Son has life; He who does not have the son of God does not have life. These things I have written to you who believe in the name of the son of God, that you may know that you have eternal life, and that you may continue to believe in the name of the son of God.

1st John 5:6-13 NKJV I did not know Him; but that He should be revealed to Israel, therefore, I came baptizing with water." i did not know Him, but He who sent me to baptize with water said to me, "Upon whom you see the Spirit descending,and remaining on Him, this is He who baptizes with the Holy Spirit"

1 John 31, 33 NKJV

JOHN BAPTIZED IN WATER BECAUSE HE DID NOT KNOW JESUS YET!

This means anyone who still baptizes in water still has not known Jesus, the One whom the Father has sent to take away the sins of the world, that He might sanctify and cleanse her with the washing of water by the word, that He might present her to Himself a glorious church. Not having spot or wrinkle, or any such thing, but that she should be holy and without blemish. Water=Word, Spirit=Salvation, Both are Jesus

WORD OF GOD AND SALVATION

Ephesians 5:26-27 Kjv: God loves you and wants you to know Him so He can fill you with peace and give you real life– forever. "God loves the people of this world so much that He gave His only Son,so that everyone who has faith in Him will have eternal life and never die." Jesus said, " I came so that everyone will have life, and have it in its fullest."

Since God planned for us to have peace and life, why are we so far fromGod? Jesus Christ is God's son. He is the only one who can bring us back to God. Jesus died on the cross and rose from the grave. He paid the penalty for our sin and bridged the gap between God and people.

"There is only one God, and Christ Jesus is the only one who can bring us to God." " Christ died for our sins. An innocent person died for those who are guilty. Christ did this to bring you to God. There is only one God, and Christ Jesus is the only one who can bring us to God." " Christ died for our sins. An innocent person died for There is only one God, and Christ Jesus is the only one who can bring us to God." " Christ died for our sins. An innocent person died for those who are guilty. Christ did this to bring you to God."

John 14:6 NKJV: Jesus said unto him, i am the way, the truth, and the life: No man cometh unto the Father, but by me. We must trust Jesus Christ to forgive our sins and receive him as our savior, and serve him as our Lord. " As many as received Him, to them He gave the right to become the sons of God, even those who believed in His name." 1 John 4:10 Nkjv: Here in His love, not that we loved God, but that He loved us, and sent His son to be the propitiation for our sins. **Jesus Christ already paid to live your life for Him.**

Faith

Part One

Faith is not JUST a WORD: "faith" is defined by God's perspective as being humble obedience to the issuance of His grace, by which ye are saved.

Let us see how this is revealed through someone everyone is well acquainted with: Abraham.

Abraham, a righteous man of God because of his faith according to the standard that God determined for righteousness at that time, in order for him to be found righteous and a man of faith. Thus righteousness was imputed upon him because of his faith.

In Genesis 12 vs. 1 – 4, God told Abram *"Get thee out of thy country, and from thy kindred, and from thy father's house, unto a land that I will show thee:"* and Abram did not enter into reason with God, neither did he doubt the Lord, but Abram reacted and *"So Abram departed, as the Lord had spoken unto him:"* Abram left his birth country and all he knew, took everything he owned and his wife Sara, including Lot and left. He didn't leave a door open for his return to that which *he knew*, because he followed instruction from the Lord and *obeyed*.

Abraham in the presence of grace OBEYED the *word* that God had spoken to him.

Moving forward, we see in Gen 15 vs.1 – 6, that the word of God came to Abraham in a vision and thus, the Lord made him a promise that his seed would be as the number of the stars, uncountable. Thus, Abraham even having no child from his union with Sara, at the high age of 75, didn't doubt God for one moment, but it is written, *"And he believed in the Lord,"* and then due to his *believe*, the following happened, *"and he (God) accounted it to him for righteousness"*

We can therefore see the established pattern for being found righteous before God, which is grace + faith = righteousness, of which, Faith is the response of a believer in obedience to grace. Grace is the form of communication received from God, it is His voice, His power by which He reveals Himself to believers as their Creator, making them aware of their longing to know Him and thus to seek Him and join themselves to Him. By grace they are sustained and nurtured to become fruitful and build the House of the Lord.

Faith is the word that identifies the heart's humble response to grace on hearing the truth (knowledge) of God, which is Jesus Christ our Lord.

Faith is to BELIEVE.

Believing IN what is heard, and thus to acknowledge Jesus Christ(truth) as the pattern and record for faith, to mold with the knowledge through labor with the tokens provided by God for faith's expression and to submit to the effectual power of the Holy Spirit, which is the Spirit of Truth.

Faith worketh trust in God, for in as much as Satan as the father of lies, deceived men to believe that the promises of God can be attained whilst remaining independent from God, by believing in many truths (doctrines of men), so God has provided a remedy called Truth (Jesus Christ = knowledge of God=gospel of salvation), that reunites the obedient with God and joins them to Him as they are rooted in Christ (abide), the offense (breach) being removed that exists between God and man due to sin and death. Equity is restored and peace rules the heart.

This meaning Christ Jesus rules in peace within and manifests His peace for overcoming the contradictions to be endured and suffered through the process of transforming the old man unto the new man.

The definition of faith is: Man's obedience to the grace of God, as grace is initiated (given/issued/poured out) by God, to call man from darkness unto His Light. Therefore grace calls man to recognize Him in truth and to accept Him in truth as the heart is humbled by grace in that moment of revelation.

Therefore, faith is obedience to the impact of grace, whereby the heart is *humbled* to grace and yield to the *will of God* and thereafter *submits* to the effectual working power of the Holy Spirit within, through due process, who confirms and bears witness to Jesus Christ in truth, as the foundation knowledge is laid within the heart through re-education of the mind (renewing of the mind) from laboring with false knowledge (which is the deception of Satan) unto laboring with truth (knowledge of Christ) that forms the mind of Christ within, which means being "like-minded" - having the mind of Christ, which means to "see" through the eyes of Christ, which means to have His perspective. This is the perspective of the Throne and thus, this IS what it means to be a true Christian. It means to be "Christ-like". Not referring to His outward appearance or by acting as He would have done in scenarios, but in fact, to HAVE the MIND of Christ Jesus. By His perspective faith is perfect as the believer is then perfect IN and THROUGH Him. Can you see this?

Grace awakens the soul to seek God, to want to know God on acceptance of grace that calls man from out of darkness (ignorance=death and sin) unto His marvelous light (truth=life and virtue through fruit bearing) whereby the face of God is revealed in and by truth. Meaning, God is seen in all things as the Spirit is the witness of Jesus Christ in truth. Can you see this? "Darkness' ' means spiritual ignorance whereby man has been transgressing against God, walking in contradiction to His truth. Ignorance does not mean "innocence", only those that accept Christ in truth remaining in covenant return to innocence like little children (pure and undefiled conscience), but those who reject His grace and covenant terms, are grace resisters (resisting Him) and are deemed sinners, sinning against God wilfully and thus by choice. Man has been given a sovereign will, free will, by which he can determine whether he wants to yield to the will of God and thus express his love to God by choice through obedience in faith, or to turn away from God and walk after his own imaginations and the traditions he has grown accustomed too, that strokes the ego, boosts the carnal mind in thinking he can live a life separately from God by own strength to confirm the self and build a kingdom for the self on earth whilst making God subject to his own will.

There are just two choices, no sitting on the fence, accept grace or reject it.

With both choices there are subsequent rewards and a kingdom, an inspiration, knowledge and wisdom embraced and fruit bearing that will take place. The choice remains with the believer which road he/she will take, the broad or the narrow way, because there is no middle way.

Grace is God's form of communication to the soul by which He reveals Christ to the believer, thus by grace comes the revelation of Christ, by which the heart is illuminated and enlightened, as the Spirit testify of Christ in the truth heard and to awaken the heart to know God. It is at this point that a choice is made…to either accept the revelation of grace or to resist the grace of God.

In accepting the revelation of Jesus Christ in truth by grace, the believer accepts Jesus Christ as the Son of God, being God, and willingly submit his soul into the care of God for the transformation process to begin, as the heart yields to the Spirit of God that is the witness of the record of faith, which is Jesus Christ.

This means that the believer agrees to the terms of His covenant and enters into a new tradition of faith that is governed by the Law of grace and truth through the effective working power of the Spirit under His stewardship.

If a believer resists the grace of God, he will turn away from this revelation to walk after the traditions of men following the doctrine of men that stands in direct contradiction of His truth that makes him an enemy of God.

Truth offends. It cuts deep and the conscience feels convicted because of its transgression against God, because the will is weak due to sin and death.

Therefore grace = revelation = Jesus Christ. Can you see this?

Man's perception of faith is <u>NOT</u> God's perception of faith...there IS a difference. Knowing the difference is very important. If one does not know the difference, how will one know what God deems right and acceptable for faith's expression and service to Him? The things of man are NOT equal to the things of God... there IS a difference.

Darkness and Light abide not in the same space, as darkness flees before Light.

When someone says they have faith in something, someone or in a certain concept/venture/system, it's a strong belief or conviction felt by that person, that is normally strengthened by an inspired emotion or a set of principles of the self, or a group of people that's like-minded, working towards the same goal(s).

When based on/in religion, it becomes a very strong conviction and trust, that is then expressed through activities, behavior or a form of correctness in a specified way, that becomes the tradition of that specific denomination, befitting the group or denomination one is part of, that each follow their *own* understanding (private interpretation and according to <u>precept and line</u>) of scripture (text) on which <u>their</u> specific <u>doctrine</u> taught, is based..

<u>Precept and line: what does it mean?</u>

When faith is measured according to *<u>precept and line</u>* and not by the *<u>pattern</u>* of Jesus Christ, we see the *ignorance displayed* about how God <u>measures</u> faith. We read about this in Isaiah 10:13, *"But the word of the Lord was unto them precept upon precept, precept upon precept; line upon line, line upon line; here a little and there a little; that they might go, and fall backward, and be broken, and snared, and taken".*

What does it mean to regard the word of the Lord as precept and line?

Precept = scripture, the written word, paper and ink

When precept is *carnally applied* to the different areas of our lives, the flesh serves as the 'plumb line' for measuring scripture.

By this form of gospel Christians try to build faith in Christ by ordering their lives in <u>imitation</u> of Him, according to their misappropriation of scripture, rather than ordering faith according to the pattern of Jesus's truth.

1. When someone tells you to read the Bible and then to ask God what He is saying to you by that scripture and then to do it, it's an example of this form of gospel, thus *precept and line.*

By precept and line faith is *redirected to the self* instead of to Jesus Christ.

2. Another example shall be, when someone tells you to go to scripture and see what scripture says about the problem/ issue/ dilemma or sadness you experience and then to apply it to your life.

The same operation is taking place as mentioned with the first example.

Faith is <u>redirected</u> to the self for <u>resolution</u> of a problem rather than directing faith back to Jesus Christ, which means to <u>abide in Him</u> though the restricted authorized sanctified <u>activity of faith</u> as designed and given by God for His new covenant priesthood wherein God and not the self is served and worshiped.

The one thing everyone needs to understand today is that the Bible is NOT about us, it's about Jesus Christ. It's NOT a book of psychology, or a book that directs our life in better ways for peace of mind and security of life. The Bible in its whole is about HIM. The word of God is NOT precept and line, it's NOT paper and ink; He is not text nor is He the precept of scripture. He is NOT the resolution to issues of life and problems experienced, no matter what you have been taught. It's false, a false perception based on misunderstanding of the gospel and lack of direction of faith due to the loss of the eyes of the church through ordained appointed stewards of His government 2000 years ago.

Yes, it's hard to take, it may be a shock, it may seem impossible but this is unfortunately the truth of the matter. The Jesus portrayed in Christianity today, is like a Santa Claus, bringing all goodies to make you feel better, to reward you for being good and spoiling you with excitement of his coming with yet another bag of rewards for trying your best to be a good person and all you have to do, is ask and you shall receive? As with Santa Claus, it's only the children that believe he exists and they do it out of ignorance. That's what they have been told by those who know better than to tell a lie. But it makes for good feelings and companionship at a certain time of the year, everyone gets caught up in the excitement of the moment, it's then when people believe in "that there is still good' left in the world and are united in the good intentions of those feelings. Jesus Christ was not sent to the world to make us feel good and better about ourselves, nor to be the One that will solve all our problems and issues at hand whenever we feel like asking for help and a miracle. He was not sent to be subject to us, or to be placed in a closet until we remember Him in need and out of desparacy. Then again to be rejected when our prayers aren't answered in our own time and things go not go according to our expectations or to be praised when things do work right for us, seeing it as the Hand of God in His will for our lives. Can you see that this is the way He has been abused by Christians?

But also the tellers of lies (*preachers of false gospel*) have been lied to (*snared, broken, taken through false knowledge = false doctrine*), they think it's acceptable (*because it looks like Christ, its taken from scripture*) to spread a lie(*teachings and preaching of ministers of false gospel in denominational churches*) and give life to it (*zeal through passion of Christ; gospel dressed with a different jacket for each generation and upcoming needs of believers*), its what they know and have been taught to believe when they were but children(*following the traditions and doctrines of men*), so the cycle is never ending(*deep darkness prevails= ignorance*), through generation upon generation, it grows in momentum(*rise of mega ministries*), in zeal and in opulence (*power of 'faith' to those who walk in false knowledge, which is not the Spirit of God giving witness to Christ*).

Now, liken that to the church of today, the same mode of operation (*deception of Satan; contorting the truth to dish up a truth to suit the needs of man and to sympathize with the frailty of man – the flesh - his issues and needs of life; deception through lies told*), a lie told (*believe in Christ the way you want to, its acceptable; God accepts you as you are and knows your heart; precept and line denominations*) That is the same with Christians, they believe what they have been taught out of ignorance, they know no better, but it's not excusing them, as the truth of the Lord has been revealed in these last days by His stewards and servants of truth to the world.

Therefore, let's recap:

Precept and line is NOT truth but another gospel preached. Can you see that??

Jesus Christ is the LIVING WORD of God; He is the Steward of His Grace and Truth.

Christians try to lay claim to the promises of Jesus Christ by precept rather than covenant, because all they can see is the *themes and issues of life* as Christ is *obscured* from the gospel they embrace.

In reality, Christians measure their obedience to God by *precept of scripture*, the precept gospel, and fall victim to following <u>another</u> <u>Jesus</u>, which means a <u>gospel</u> <u>that is *contrary* to Christ's gospel of</u> <u>truth</u>, and work to order their faith by the *power of reason and human logic* to direct human principle after the wisdom of the world.

Because of the darkened soul, there is a great *misconception* regarding righteousness, the righteousness of God is something totally different from what Christians have been taught, as is the understanding of *grace, faith, righteousness, justification, sanctification, holiness, peace, rest, truth, charity, regeneration and renewing of the mind.* All needed for understanding of the gospel of Christ and for the process of transformation of the soul from darkness unto light, the old man to the new man, and thus for the rebirth of the old man unto the new man that is the birth of Christ within, which is the virtue of Christ formed within that makes the soul pleasing and acceptable to the Lord.

There is a misconception due to precepts, regarding righteousness, due to the soul being exposed to false knowledge (knowledge of the world) that removes faith from the heart, *redirecting* faith to *the self* rather than to Christ as the *contact point-, record- and pattern of faith.*

The righteousness of God is Jesus Christ, not the precept of scripture. Jesus Christ is the measure of faith; He is the righteousness of God and the staff on which we lean.

It's by this measure that we stand before God and are accepted by Him, when righteousness is measured to Christ by the apostles' doctrine(Acts 2 :41), then Christians are established, strengthened and settled (rooted) in Him (1 Peter.5:10), but when faith is by precept and line, then they are snared, broken and taken (Is.28:13), trying to fit the *moral center* to the *precept for righteousness*, because rather than seeing Jesus Christ they see the image of the self, termed *"self-righteousness'*.

By grace we are saved by faith, having met the standard of Jesus Christ, which is revealed in the truth of the gospel that is called "holy knowledge".

Faith

Part 2

The tradition of Jesus Christ =The tradition of the true gospel of Jesus Christ

Let's follow the path of the Spirit as He leads us to understanding what faith in Jesus is, how to *abide* in Him and how to *partake* of Him through faith.

When the doctrine of God, which is His knowledge through Jesus Christ, the gospel, is taken into many different directions, it's not His doctrine (knowledge) anymore, for then His doctrine takes on another meaning, another form and thus another Jesus is formed through the imagination (the mind of man works with imagery) and zeal of religious men/women that each understand through private interpretation, teach, preach and belief what they believe to be true of Jesus Christ, as the TRUTH.

Although they use scripture as a reference point and the basis of what they believe in, it's not the truth (doctrine) of God anymore.

Evidence of the Knowledge having been changed, is in the following: when the FOCUS of faith is not ON Christ Jesus in truth, serving Him by works of faith (spiritual works), but the focus is turned AWAY from Jesus Christ onto THE SELF and serving Him with works of the flesh..

Jesus Christ is the HUB of true faith; He is the center of our attention. We were created BY God FOR God, not God for us

The Oxford dictionary gives a spot on description of the word "focus":

[Focuses]

1: the distance from an eye or lens at which an object appears clearest.

2: something that is the center of interest or attention etc. [Focused/ focusing]

1. Use or adjust a lens so that the object appears clearly

2. Concentrate (focusing attention)

1. When the focus of a lens (perspective) is out, the image seen is out of focus and is not clear (true). That is what happened to believers by the gospel embraced and taught today. The image (gospel = Jesus Christ) is not seen (discerned spiritually) clear(true), so now the mind(intellect) works with(mold with) what it knows(false knowledge: traditions of man) and have as a reference point(private interpretation), in expectation that the image(gospel) the lens(perspective) is focused on should be the image of the object(Jesus Christ) its focused on, but because there is a lack of knowledge in obtaining clarity, there is no clarity of the image. The true clear image is obscured due to the focus being out.

All that's needed is for a lens to be tuned incorrectly, for the focus to be unclear and clouded. What is then seen is not the object in its clarity, but the mind compensates for this lack by filling in the gaps drawing from the knowledge it embraces. The focus of attention is on an unclear image accepted to be what is believed to be the object of the desire. The expectation is based on what one perceives to be true, and not the truth.

The perspective of man is molded from the fabric of the flesh, thus carnal, but when the spiritual law of grace and truth are embraced through obedience in faith with the spiritual things of God, and then the perspective of man changes, as the mind is transformed from being carnally minded to being spiritually minded. The spiritual minded take on the likeness of Christ within the mind, that sees Jesus Christ clearly in all things revealed and witnessed by the Holy Spirit, and their perspective is then of The Throne(God) not of the flesh. As the perspective changes, so does the appetite of man changes. The appetite changes from the desire to be fed by the substance of the flesh, to being fed by the substance of Jesus Christ that brings life to the soul.

2. When Jesus Christ is the <u>center of our attention</u>, then He is our heart's desire. He becomes the affection of our hearts.

Now it doesn't mean that believers do not have the desire to please the Lord. Many desire to please Him and thus strive to appease Him by works that they think will be acceptable to the Lord. But the thing is, the perspective of man is formed due to misunderstanding of the truth and embracing the doctrines of men that have placed the focus on man and not on God through Jesus Christ, therefore Jesus is not the center of attention, but man is. How is this true? Well, it's evident through "precept and line", as discussed in part 1 of Faith. Through precept and line the believer perceives that Jesus is the one to go to when in need of resolving issues and circumstances. To confirm this perspective, believers quote Matthew 7 vs.7 to confirm this mindset, *"Ask, and it shall be given you; seek, and ye shall find; knock, and it shall be opened unto you."* Interpreted carnally, Jesus is the resolution to all problems, but This speaks not of the aspiration of man to gain resolve and outcome for his needs, circumstance and issues of life, but speaks of gaining the things of God's kingdom through embracing His truth through faiths labor with the tokens he has sanctified for faith by the blood of Christ Jesus, whilst conforming to truth.

For it is written, *"But seek ye first the kingdom of God, and his righteousness; and all these things shall be added unto you."* (Matt 6 vs.33) Jesus Christ has to be the focus of our attention and then shall the Lord add unto the faithful all else, for the Lord takes into His care (mercy) those who accept Him in His covenant and abide in Him. In Matt 6 vs 34, He says, *"Take therefore no thought for the morrow; for the morrow shall take thought for the things of itself. Sufficient unto the day is the evil thereof."* The Lord knoweth what we need but first we have to be obedient to Him and reciprocate faith and a willingness to be joined to Him by the terms He has set for salvation in covenant through Jesus Christ our Lord.

Jesus Christ is not the solution to man's problems, but the remedy given by God for our salvation, He is the truth, the way and the light.

When Jesus is the center of our attention, the spiritual eyes are turned upward and He is kept in sight at all times as the obedient walk in His light, doing the things that please Him and join them to Him. Jesus covers the breach that exists between God and man due to sin through false knowledge.

When Jesus is the center of a believer's attention, then there will be consistency through laboring with the knowledge of God, with the tokens of faith's expression remaining within the restrictions He has set. This labor begets trust in God, as He is faithful and righteous in all His ways.

When Jesus Christ is the center of our attention, then we receive His spiritual blessings, enter into His fullness and are sustained daily by grace to increase with virtue through fruit bearing, taking on His likeness and image, as we drink from the living waters that flow forth from Above.

By works of the flesh, believers seek God's approval and seek to appease Him through the traditions of men, that are initiated, designed and implemented by religious men *(under <u>inspiration</u> of the prince of the air/antichrist spirit/Satan: Eph 2:2)* and followed by believers that attend these denominational churches in the hope of having an experience of faith by which they can know and feel that they walk in the *way of the Lord*, thinking they are experiencing the presence of the Lord.

This "changed knowledge", is presented as the gospel of Christ, whilst they boast of knowing and understanding His truth.

God approves only of Jesus Christ as the acceptable sacrifice, spotless and perfect. It was Jesus that died and was resurrected by the power of God, so that all who believe in His Name may be saved.

It is by His measure that we will be weighed and found acceptable or not. Adamites have nothing to offer God that is equal to Jesus Christ through and in whose plan for our salvation was designed, initiated and fulfilled.

Anything less than Christ (truth) is unacceptable and nothing more than Christ is needed, because Jesus Christ was/is perfect in all His ways. There is nothing lacking in God's plan for salvation and He is not in need of our input to make it more perfect.

In other words, nothing added, nothing taken away from the gospel of Christ is needed for salvation through Jesus Christ.

When men offer God more OR less than Jesus Christ, it speaks of something that is not OF Him. Something is missing. Something has changed.

When truth is molded into another doctrine, it's not truth anymore, for it speaks of another perspective that is not His perspective.

Then it's NOT the gospel of Jesus, but a gospel that is OF men, following the traditions of men, according to the rudiments of the world.

In 2 Thessalonians 2:15, the Apostle Paul said, *"Therefore brethren, stand fast, and hold the traditions which ye have been taught, whether by word or our epistle."*

What were they teaching believers?

The true gospel of Jesus Christ: The Truth of God.

Apostle Paul said, *"...the traditions"* they have been taught, which is: THE tradition of the gospel of Jesus Christ.

This tradition, by which faith is made perfect IN (abiding) and THROUGH(washing action of Truth for purging, cleansing and healing by the Spirit of grace) Jesus Christ, and the death of the old man(flesh) unto a new man(spiritual), in whom IS born the product of the *substance of Jesus Christ*, which is His virtue through fruit-bearing. The *fruit* reflects *the Giver*: Jesus Christ. Virtue is Jesus Christ formed within those, who believe in His gospel by the Spirit of Truth, and follow the authorized activity of faith for divine transformation of the soul whilst rooted in Him, partaking of Him daily, forsaking the self(dying to the flesh) and being subject to Him.

Thus, the apostles taught those who believed in His truth, *the tradition of faith* by which those that BELIEVED could abide in Him and partake of Him, experiencing the fullness of Christ daily.

Faith

Part 3

The tradition of Jesus Christ =The tradition of the true gospel of Jesus Christ

The following was given through the inspiration of the Holy Spirit and speaks about God's design for faith and the condition of the church.

Let them who have eyes to see, see and ears to hear, hear by the grace of God.

"A Potter created a vase from a lump of clay on his potter wheel; He created it according to his <u>own specifications</u>. At completion of his project he stands back and is <u>filled with joy</u> at his handiwork that <u>reflects his own creativity</u> (1). He leaves his vase in the care of a student as he sets off towards home. The student oversee the care of the vase in due diligence, keeping it as is and where it was left in the room (2) but in comes another student, not being of the same mind and seeing the vase in all its beauty, but not understanding the perfection of the vase, he seeks to find fault with it, under protest of the diligent and faithful student, the second student proceeds to prod and press the vase, leaving his own fingerprints on the vase. The potters' fingerprints were wiped away, which gave the vase its unique beauty in appearance and form, thus the perfection of the vase in form and beauty was changed irrevocably. The transgressor stands in boastful pride, seeing now his own reflection of perfection in the vase, he leaves the shocked student who was in appreciation and admiration

*of the pure beauty of the vase as it was created by the potter(3). The student decides to guard the vase until the potter returns to ensure that nothing else happens to it. (4) On the return of the potter the next morning(5) he found the student asleep in the room and then saw the altered condition of the vase. It did not resemble the vase as he created it. There was no trace of the beauty created by his own fingerprints and perfection of form in which it was created by him (6). He grew increasingly wrathful and turned to the student who awoke from his slumber(7). The student smiled at him and said, "Master, I can <u>remember</u> the beauty and perfection that you created that vase with, I will keep it in remembrance all my days. For that vase, has been <u>etched in my heart</u> and I can never forget <u>the glory</u> thereof. I am <u>inspired by you</u> to reach that same perfection by my <u>labor</u> with the same clay that you created it from, but please do <u>instruct me and council me</u> so that <u>I will not create what I will but what you have created in perfection, so that it will glorify your craftsmanship through my labor</u>(8). For I do as you will." (9) The potter felt his anger subdued and in long suffering and patience led the student to a cabinet on the wall. He said, "In this cabinet is my will for you (*Jesus Christ=Truth of God=contact point for faith*), and that is that you will reach the same perfection (*rebirth = perfection that reflects Christ within, as faith is made perfect through Him*) through my tutorship, I will teach you all my ways(*path of righteousness, walking upright before the Lord*) and make my craftsmanship(*operation of God upon the heart to bring forth divine change*) perfect in you, so that all who sees your works(*works of the Spirit*), will know you are a product of my craftsmanship and tutorage(*being of Him, being called Sons of God, by their fruits they shall be known*). By your works shall I be known by you(*through obedience in faith the righteous shall behold the kingdom of God, they shall see the face of God in all things*), and you shall be known to be of me: A student of my ways.(*a holy nation, a peculiar people*) The beauty and perfection that I see will be what you see (*being like minded, having the mind of Christ: renewing of the mind*) and it will be laid in your* *heart*(the commandments of the Lord written upon the table of the heart), *so that you can bring forth fruits*(virtue) *that resemble my power*(Jesus) *to empower*(by the law of grace and truth) *those whom can see the perfection of what I have created for you to labor and increase with, for it was my own intention that only Those who could observe the perfection of what I created, shall be taught of me to be students worthy of my power*(predestined, called and chosen unto righteousness by the will of God). *But he that changed the perfection and beauty of my creation(vase) he too shall be known by his works*(grace resisters, the corrupted and unfaithful), *for it shall reflect his evil eye*(darkness, by their fruit they shall be known) *that defaced*(changed truth, smited the face of Christ) *what was perfect and he shall walk in the boast of his own perception of what beauty and perfection is* (walk in derision: confounded in his own logic and separated from His light), *to destruction shall it lead him*(death unto death), *for he shall neither enter into my power, neither shall he experience the joy*(the desire of wanting to do the will of God) *of being taught by me in my ways*(righteousness), *for his ways is evil*(faithlessness, darkness through false knowledge) *and single, focused on creating by his own will what he sees as beauty and perfection*(traditions of men/ doctrines of men), *but his mind is not my mind and his joy is short lived, for he shall not be known by me as he shall not know me.*

In the cabinet (restrictions given for faith, the terms of His covenant) *was a vase* (record and pattern for faith=Jesus Christ) *equal to the one the potter created, the one he kept hidden from eyes* (carnal eyes and the imagination of man) *and safe from destruction*(keeping it pure and not to be changed), *only the student taught by him*(called and chosen, obedient to grace, the faithful), *could observe*(spiritually minded) *that vase as it was hidden from all who could not observe its perfection and beauty."* (10)

(1) Christ Jesus is the <u>perfect design of God for faith</u>. Jesus Christ is the Truth of God as the perfect creative 'handiwork' of God to

fulfill the <u>perfect design of God</u> (truth=knowledge of God=truth) for salvation through Him: For God has set *everything* that is needed for faith's labor and expression WITHIN Jesus Christ by which faith is made perfect. Yes! Faith can be perfect WHEN the expression of faith, the knowledge embraced, the Spirit that empowers faith and fruit born within meets God's expectation by His terms. Thus, for faith to be *perfect*, the believer has to enter INTO Christ, thus ABIDE IN Him and is therefore hidden in Him by remaining within the restrictions set for faith in Jesus Christ. We abide IN Him when the tokens of the covenant as given by God is used in faiths labor knowing and upholding *the terms* He has given for covenant faith, doing <u>works of the Spirit</u>, to *conform* to His truth and to experience the power of His grace and truth daily for transformation of the soul unto the new man. Jesus Christ is the joy of His Father and that joy is fulfilled in and partaken of by those who abide in Him, for the joy of the Lord is the reflection (virtue) of His Son within those whom love Him through Christ in obedience to His grace and conformity to His truth (knowledge).

(2) Here is brought to mind, the beginning of the Church (1st student) under stewardship of His chosen stewards, the apostles, that were the eyes of the body and oversaw the function of the faith of the body, keeping the church in remembrance of their responsibility towards God in covenant, giving direction for faith by them teaching the pure and wholesome doctrine of Jesus to the body and thus through growth in the body, all stewarded His grace that bound the body through the fellowship of charity that is the expression of Christ Jesus – who is the love of God. The church beheld Christ in all things and their faith was pleasing to the Lord.

Col 3:14 –15: *"And above all these things put on charity, which is the bond of perfectness. And let the peace of God rule in your hearts, to which also ye are called in one body; and be ye thankful."*

(3) The 2nd student represents the church after stewardship of apostles was lost to the church and man's imagination entered into faith, which means that many different interpretations of the word of God developed into diverse doctrines that became traditions of the church, therefore the church was divided and not in unity anymore, that speaks of embracing one truth, one faith and one Spirit; the pure perfection of the truth (gospel) was changed by believers into something unrecognizable. It did not represent the original design for faith anymore, the focus shifted to the self rather than Jesus Christ through sprouting of denominational churches, each with their own truth and belief. Therefore the beauty of the fruits of faith by the law of grace and truth was replaced by the corrupted fruits of iniquity by the law of death and sin that resulted in the soul remaining in a state of darkness and the defiled conscience carrying the burden of condemnation under the law. The design for faith (Jesus Christ) now represented the image (simulated version of Jesus Christ) that man created for faith that confirmed his own idea (through interpretation of scripture/precept and line) of what was perfect and beautiful (doctrines and traditions of men). Man now walked in his own boast of perfecting faith by his own standard that confirmed only his own fallen nature by embracing false knowledge.

(4) This brings to mind the following: that even the zeal and good intentions of those of faith cannot bring perfection to faith when faith is not according to God's standard in the absence of His grace and truth (spiritual law of His covenant). When truth becomes error, those that follow the error as the truth, are also in error, for there is no light in darkness and no innocence because of ignorance. Isaiah 5 vs. 20 was brought to remembrance, *"Woe unto them that call evil good, and good evil; that put darkness for light, and light for darkness; that put bitter for sweet and sweet for bitter!"*

The truth is seen as from the adversary and his knowledge seen as truth, for it's what man has embraced through doctrines and traditions of men. Satan has led man to believe that God's knowledge is evil and should be wary off, when it contradicts what has been taught in churches today, in the absence of Jesus' stewardship over His church.

For would Satan want man to know the truth and inherit eternal life?

If a farmer decides to produce a NEW variation apple from the "Granny Smith" - that has a sour taste and green skin but on consumption leaves a bitter sweet taste on the tongue – and to maintain the 'eye appeal' of it (recognized green color) in order to market that new green apple so that it will appeal to a bigger market due to the new altered taste, it is not the same apple, is it?

It may look the same but it has been altered and tastes differently, a taste that will appeal to everyone. The same has been done to the knowledge of God. Can you see this?

(5) Restoration of the Church to the Truth of God, through stewardship and in His priesthood, which is also the day of the Lord's visitation to His church for the church to be made perfect through Jesus Christ. Thus the church is returned to beauty (virtue born within the soul through the operation of God upon the soul) and power (law of grace and truth), knowing the fear of God (which means fairing separation from God's grace by which those of faith are sustained, nurtured and increased). This means that God has *restored* the knowledge of Jesus Christ in its pureness to the church through His stewards of truth, in order for believers to walk in the power of faith that pleases Him.

This is the time in which the church is united in one Spirit and one Truth, in one mind and bound together through the *charity* that is the end product of faith's labor. *Charity* is the expression of Jesus Christ verbally, that is a gift given back to God that

He accepts, and finds pleasing since it reflects the knowledge of Jesus Christ.

(6) This speaks of the church being put to sleep (slumber) through false knowledge, and thus needed to be awakened by the presence of the Lord. The soul is awakened by grace from out of its deep sleep, to recognize and embrace the truth on the impact of grace.

Interesting is the definition given by the <u>Oxford dictionary</u> for "sleep": "The condition or time of rest in which the eyes are closed, the body relaxed, and the mind unconscious."

This really explains it well. For this is exactly what happened to the church after truth was lost to the church. God designed our souls to *increase* with *His own knowledge(truth)*, therefore one can determine that when God gave His knowledge for us to *increase* with, then knowledge not given by Him, will obviously have the opposite effect, it will *decrease* the soul.

His knowledge brings beauty (virtue) to the soul that will transform the soul to reflect a mirror image of Jesus Christ, - and then obviously one can also determine that the opposite is going to happen when false knowledge is embraced for faith. Can you see this?

And who opposes God? Who wants to steal faith away from God? Who wants all men to fall and be damned eternally? The answer we all know...Satan, the adversary to truth (Jesus Christ).

1 Peter 5:8: *"Be sober, be vigilant; because your adversary the devil, as a roaring lion, walketh about, seeking whom he may devour:"*

Satan wants his own mirror image to be formed within every soul, because he knows that this is not the acceptable image that will enable one to be found approved of God.

Satan wants to be the mold of your perception (mindset and thought patterns); he wants to see himself reflected in us (fruits of iniquity). He wants to prove to God that we are not worthy of salvation (by tempting man to fall according to the way of the aspiration of man and being a sympathizer of man's fallen nature; A nature that he initiated and facilitated), even though God gave us the remedy to Satan's error, Jesus Christ. Satan is a diligent worker and promoter of his own knowledge, and ever present to steal faith from the heart and to offer us false promises of peace and glory and a shortcut to divinity by sidestepping God's requirements for returning to perfection through Jesus Christ, presenting himself as our savior.

(7) "awoke from his slumber" – When grace is initiated by God to call all unto Him, those whom accept His grace, awake from 'sleep' (darkness which means ignorance) and enter into His light, as the spiritual eyes are opened to behold all things of His kingdom and the ears are opened to the inspiration of God's Spirit.

(8) *"remember"*

Mark 8:18: *"Having eyes, see ye not? and having ears, hear ye not? And do you not remember?"*

The things of God cannot be seen by the carnal mind, but is beheld in all its glory by the spiritually minded.

Man has always known that he was destined for 'greater things' and therefore strives to attain it through his talents and gifts given unto him for completion and fulfillment of his life on earth, but we cannot achieve perfection of faith by these things, only through Jesus Christ will we be perfect before the Lord. But man has forgotten the origin of his creation and walked contrary to God due to sin and death as he slumbered till awakened by grace. So when grace awakens man to see God in truth, the lie he believed (darkness = false knowledge) and knew as the truth, has no hold on him anymore, for he shall behold the kingdom of God in all things by the grace of God and the power of His Spirit.

Isaiah 35:5: *"Then the eyes of the blind shall be opened, and the ears of the deaf shall be unstopped."*

Matthew 13:16: *"But blessed are your eyes, for they see: and your ears, for they hear."* *"keep it in remembrance"*

Through diligence and consistency at the altar of Christ, the righteous are kept in remembrance of their responsibility to God and keep His commandments as they keep in remembrance(reflect on/ think on/mold with) the knowledge of Jesus Christ.

When they do this, they are obedient in faith and this is pleasing to the Lord.

"etched in my heart" God writes His commandments on the tables of the heart and the affection of the heart is then Jesus Christ, as the appetite changes from that which is of the world to that which is of the Spirit.

"I can never forget <u>the glory</u> thereof..." The glory of God is Jesus Christ. As the new man is reborn from the clay of the old man, the virtue of Christ is born within through the process of fruit bearing (regeneration). Virtue is the glory of God and thus the righteous before the Lord, glorify Him by the very substance of Christ that is born within the soul. John 15: 8: *"herein is my father glorified, that ye bear much fruit;"*

"inspired" The Holy Spirit is the inspiration of God, that is the power of God that bears witness to Jesus Christ in truth, by grace. The faithful are inspired by the power of God to seek the Lord with all their heart, soul, mind and strength. (Mark 12:30)

This is the 1st commandment of the Lord, given unto those who serve Him in Spirit and truth, doing righteousness, as the second commandment is, "Thou shalt love thy neighbor as thyself." (Mark 12:31) The 2nd speaks of charity. We love one another by charity, for charity covers a multitude of sins.

"labor" Speaks of our activity of faith with the given knowledge and tokens of His covenant.

"instruct me and counsel me" Instruction in the knowledge of God. The Holy Spirit draws from the foundation of knowledge that is laid within the heart through study of His knowledge, in order for the believer to increase in knowledge and understanding that begets wisdom that is not earthbound. The Spirit makes connections from the knowledge laid within, to reveal the mystery of Christ that has been hidden from the carnal eye, unto the spiritually minded.

Phil 4:12: *"...ever where and in all things I am instructed both to be full* (fullness of Christ) *and to be hungry* (desire to know God and increase with Him within), *both to abound* (to increase with grace unto growth and faith) *and to suffer need* (dying of the self),"

Those of the Spirit walketh not after the counsel of men, nor after their own counsel, for the heart is a deceiver and the imagination evil, but walketh after the counsel of Him that loved them first.

"glorify your craftsmanship through my labor" The Lord is glorified through the birth of the new man, for the new man is the mirror image of His Son, who is the measure and weight for being accepted by God. Therefore the virtue born within is a testimony to the power of God to bring forth divine change through His divine power.

1 Cor 6:20: *"For ye are bought with a price: therefore glorify God in your body, and in your spirit, which are God's."*

(9) In the presence of grace the heart is humbled, and the will strengthened, to do the will of God.

The Holy Spirit empowers faith and makes faith living, even as faith needs work. Works are needed to express faith with. By works fruit is born that reflects the giver of that fruit, either the adversary or God.

Faith needs knowledge for works to take place and fruit to be born, either that of darkness or that of light.

For if believers knew His knowledge and knew how to abide in Him, keeping the commandments of the Lord for His spiritual covenant of faith, they would see Him in all things and would know error from truth, and not embrace error as truth.

In 1 Cor 8:1 – 2 we read,

"Now as touching things offered unto idols, we know that we all have knowledge. Knowledge puffeth up, but charity edifieth. And if any man thinks that he knoweth anything, he knoweth nothing yet as he ought to know."

It's very easy to understand that if something is not the truth, then it must be false.

We can then safely say that any gospel preached that is not the Truth is false and therefore its false knowledge.

The gospel that is not Truth, points to the self and sympathizes with the fallen nature of man; his basic needs, his issues and struggles of life. What he needs and wants.

Such a gospel is created when believers interpret the spiritual things of God by the carnal mind, using their reason and logic to understand spiritual things without the Spirit as the witness of Christ. The Spirit will only give witness to Christ Jesus and not enter into giving witness to man, or any simulated version of Jesus created through corruption of His truth into a version that does not reflect Jesus Christ as the Word of God, the Truth and the perfect Lamb slain for the sins of the world.

Faith

Part 4

The tradition of Jesus Christ =The tradition of the true gospel of Jesus Christ

<u>The fallen nature of man</u> reflects his *fall from the glory of God*, being separated from the *light and covering of God's counsel* and thus being made *subject to darkness*, that follows *the law of death and sin*. The 1st Adam turned aside the counsel of God, to listen to the counsel of Satan, that inflamed in him the desire to seek the promises of God by *aspiration* rather than by *faith*.

For as much as Satan fell by the way of his aspiration in his attempt to attain the power and glory of God's Throne, so did he awaken that aspiration in Adam, to seek a shortcut to divinity and the promises of God, by his own measure and not the measure given by God for faith in Him.

The nature that we have grown accustomed to and have accepted as being that of being "a human" reflects the presence of death and our bondage to sin, that also bears witness to our inability to overcome either. The conscience is defiled and the will is weakened due to the effect of sin on the soul. By following the law of the flesh, the conscience is under constant condemnation (being judged by the law), always in remembrance of past sins and experiencing the need to continuously repent because of it, the heart fearing the judgments of God as the soul recognises its fallen condition.

The nature of man is likened to that of a beast of the field, thus the *beastly nature* that is the nature of *the carnal man*, walking on all fours; the eyes of the beast is turned downwards in search of food for the belly, thus fed from *the soil (the flesh)*, motivated by *instinct* for survival.

Thus, the carnal man (natural man) is driven by instinct and not by faith, but the spiritual man that has been strengthened, nurtured and sustained by grace and truth, to stand upright before God, behold Him in all His glory. The drive of the soul of the carnal man is his aspiration as he is Not being fed by the substance of the flesh, he seeks to die rather than live (spiritually), which means he willingly die to that which has come between him and God through his birth into death and sin, on entering His covenant.

People confess daily to their inability to overcome sin and that they love God, that they seek Him and then they find a church to join that confirms what they think is true, as the form of doctrine taught in that church makes them feel at home with this church.

Ever heard of the saying, "birds of a feather, flock together"?

Hereby, in context of what is being explained: Those who are like-minded, who think the same, who do the same, they who embrace the same traditions and are in one mind of what is being taught in the doctrine of that church. They tend to stand in unified agreement on what they think is right and true but still each pulls their separate way, no true unity in the congregation or amongst themselves. In the congregations of men, strife, conflict and confusion rules, not the unity and peace of Christ Jesus.

Unfortunately, they also stay spiritually hungry and thirsty, thus the bread of life (unleavened bread) and living water is absent from their faith and their faith is in vain, for no transformation of the old to the new man is taking place.

To their own distress and growing frustration, they still have the same bad habits, no lasting changes within the heart, even if they wilfully change behavior, speech or a lifestyle to adopt a form of holiness, godliness or faithfulness, they still feel condemned by their sinfulness, they still have the same struggles in overcoming their sinful nature and they still carry on searching, albeit they are in a church that makes them feel good for the duration of attending sermons.

In 1 Colossians 2:8 we read," *Beware lest any man spoil you through philosophy and vain deceit, after the tradition of men, after the rudiments of the world, and not after Christ."*

Think on this: If a dog should suddenly start to meow like a cat, it doesn't make the dog a cat, just a dog that is able to meow LIKE a cat. It might *SOUND* like a cat, but it REMAINS a dog. It has the voice of a cat, and the body of a dog. It will still have the *HABITS* of a dog, because the *HABITS ARE NOW A PART OF ITS NATURE*. The voice (adopted and wilfully changed to appear Christ-like) can't change the dog's behavior (carnal man =carnal nature) nor can the voice change the dog's physical appearance (from old man to new man). Man can try to change himself and adopt certain behavior patterns to present him changed, but only God can change the heart and soul of man through His power of regeneration, that forms the temperament of Christ within, through obedience in faith. The habit of the natural man is empowered and sustained by the power that inspires him to walk carnally and so can it be said of the spiritual man; his habit of faith is inspired by the Holy Spirit, as the old man is reborn unto the new man. The habit is taken on (formed) by the appetite for the kingdom we embrace. Can you see this?

There is only *ONE Spirit* that works with the *knowledge (doctrine) of God* and that is His own Spirit. His Spirit will work with no *OTHER* knowledge than what is given of God.

To recap, what was brought to understanding in Faith, part 3, when knowledge is changed, the Spirit will not enter into it, because that knowledge has been changed and does not resemble Jesus Christ. Remember the analogy of the Granny Smith apple? So, we now know that God's Spirit bears witness to Christ Jesus only.

Therefore, when believers change the holy knowledge into unholy knowledge, it will need a witness to give them an experience of faith. Right? <u>There are 2 kingdoms at war</u>: That which is of darkness and that which is of Light.

God provides <u>His witness</u> through <u>His Spirit</u> that bears witness of Christ (record of faith=Jesus Christ).

Satan provides his witness, that works through the 'voice' of man's own record, that will seek to benefit the prince of darkness as he promotes his own truth and sympathizes with the nature of man (fallen nature) through the altered knowledge that is under his inspiration, the spirit of the antichrist.

In TRUTH there is no error: shades of gray speak of the presence of darkness. The boast and pride of man is evident in the form of knowledge preached, as it points to man and not Christ Jesus.

God's doctrine confirms only Jesus Christ in perfection, as the Spirit of God bears witness to Jesus Christ.

The Spirit reveals Jesus to those who do the will of God in righteousness. They who know the doctrine will know the Son and so will know the Father, for Jesus did not give His doctrine of His own will, but was sent by God to do His will.

In John 7:16 – 18, we read:

"Jesus answered them, and said, My doctrine (truth) is not mine but his (God) that sent me.

If any man will do his (God) will, he shall know of the doctrine (truth), whether it be of God, or whether I speak of myself (thus saying, 'the witness of the Spirit shall testify of Me, whether I follow His will or my own').

He that speaketh of himself (after his own imagination/traditions and doctrine) *seeketh his own glory* (honor, fulfillment and completion by the aspiration): *but he that seeketh his (God) glory that sent him (Jesus), the same is true, and no unrighteousness is in him.*

AND IN John 14:24, Jesus says:

"He that loveth me not keepeth not my sayings: and the word which ye hear is not mine, but the Fathers which sent me."

Those of faith LOVE God through obedience in faith, by conforming to the doctrine(truth) of God, that is unchiseled and unchanged by the imagination of man, as they die to the natural man reborn unto the spiritual man in Christ.

2 Peter 3:18 says,

"But grow in grace, and in the knowledge of our Lord and Saviour Jesus Chris." The apostle Peter brings to understanding that we are able to GROW in grace (increase), which means grace upon grace, faith upon faith, which speaks of growth, through diligent consistent labor at the altar. Thus the more we sow, the more we grow. Amazing! As God issues grace, we reciprocate with faith and increase with His knowledge, understanding and wisdom from above regarding the connections made about the kingdom of God and discerning the opposing force, the kingdom of darkness, in which men are subject to the wiles and deception of Satan.

Thus, the apostle John also says, *"AND in the knowledge of our Lord.."* which means, growth in knowledge and that means increase with knowledge as the hidden mystery of His truth is broken open as the Spirit brings understanding and makes connections from all things revealed by the Spirit drawing from the foundation of knowledge (Jesus Christ) that is laid within the heart through Stewardship.

Like a ruminating cow, that eat and thereafter peacefully lie down or stand and re-chew what she has absorbed, extracting the substance from the grass or lucerne she has consumed, so do the faithful chew (reflect, think on, mold with) on His knowledge, gaining insight (discernment) to the 2 kingdoms at work and the things of both kingdoms as well as the inspirations (power) of both kingdoms, growing in increased understanding about the knowledge of His kingdom. The substance that is extracted from faithfully 'chewing' on the knowledge of Jesus (truth), is the substance by which the soul increases, to take on His likeness. Thus the faithful are sustained by that substance and as the cow produces milk, so do the faithful produce the 'milk' of their labor, which is called CHARITY.

In Gen 8:21 God said, *"I will not again curse the ground anymore for man's sake; for the imagination of man's heart is evil from his youth..."*

By these words, the Lord reveals and affirms that He knows the heart of man and that the heart of man is towards evil.

The word 'evil' describes the condition of man within when the truth and life of Christ is not known, embraced and not abided in, because only goodness comes by truth, for evil stands in direct contradiction to goodness.

The heart of man is inclined to evil, thus inclined to darkness, as it is devoid of the light of God.

Evil, speaks of being without truth. Can you see this?

Two words stand out from the above scriptures, the *"imagination"* and "doctrine". What happens IN the mind is manifested IN the heart and which becomes the words that one speaks. Therefore, one is KNOWN by the words one speaks. Your words reflect the kingdom you embrace.

Man's thought patterns are molded by the knowledge he accepts, since our mind works with knowledge, given life by the power of our imagination. But God is the God of knowledge which is His truth, His doctrine which is the knowledge of Jesus Christ.

We know that man is born into sin and death, into the kingdom of darkness because of the first Adam's fall. But it's only through Christ Jesus that we can be saved from darkness (ignorance: death and sin) to walk in His light (truth: life through fruit-bearing unto virtue) and so the power of man's imagination (to mold with false knowledge to project for outcome) is subdued by His truth.

For the imagination to lose its power, truth is to be known, so that the heart's affections will be directed towards God and not towards the self.

What is evident is that we need knowledge, the right knowledge (truth), for *faith* to be accepted by God.

In Hosea 4:6, God says through Hosea, *"My people are destroyed for a lack of knowledge: for thou hast rejected knowledge, I will also reject thee,"*

What knowledge did God refer to?

He referred to *His knowledge,* the knowledge of *liberty and life*: Thus, freedom from darkness and life in and through Jesus Christ.

It's only by His pure and holy knowledge that we can know the Son, and through whom all that believe in Him must enter to be received by the Father. Therefore, Jesus is the door through who one has to enter to be liberated and through who one receives life.

Why does He say "destroyed"?

When truth is absent, Jesus is absent.

When Jesus is absent, then the adversary is present. Remember, there are only two kingdoms.

When believers do not *receive* and *accept* the truth of God, they will not be accepted by the Father. God has set His plan for the salvation and redemption of mankind within Jesus Christ who is the *blueprint for faith*, the *chief cornerstone* upon which His church is built and the *High Priest* of those who abide in Him through the *works of the Spirit*.

In the absence of truth, error prevails and therefore destruction befalls the spiritually blind and deaf. They are confounded in what they believe to be true of Christ Jesus according to their own *vain imaginations*.

God has given each man a free will, to exercise by will the liberty of that will. Which means that man has the choice to be a consenter to God's plan (Truth=Jesus Christ) or a protestor, to be saved through Him or to turn away from Him. God calls all of mankind to join Him in His covenant through Jesus Christ;

He calls the poor and the weak and the weary, He calls the hungry and the destitute, He calls the rich and the famous and the mighty, but it will remain the choice of each man to whether he chooses to accept or reject the call of his/her Creator unto salvation: For all of mankind are called unto salvation, but not all will accept that invitation and gift, for not all men have faith.

In Matt 19:24 Jesus said,

"And again I say unto you, it is easier for a camel to go through the eye of a needle, than for a rich man to enter into the kingdom of God."

Word of knowledge received:

"For those rich in the things of this world, seek not the things of the Lord, but walk in proud arrogance before Him, being lord and master in their own kingdoms, they do not see the hand of God in all things pertaining to life and death, they seek not to relinquish their power to be submissive unto the Lord, for so it is in the kingdom of the Lord, that only the meek and the humble shall inherit the heavens and the earth, for the Lord resisteth the proud and accept the humble. But unto God all is possible that is impossible to man, should the heart be humbled by the power of the Spirit of grace. For it's the humble that forsake the world and return to the Lord, for it's the humble that seeketh the Lord in humble willingness to abide in Him and walk in faith's expression that is Jesus Christ our Lord. Amen."

Those whom have a full barn in the world (fattened by the knowledge and wisdom of this world that they embrace) are rich in their own boasting,

In James 4:6 we read, *"But he giveth more grace. Wherefore he saith, God resisteth the proud (those who stand in their own testimony, those who are resisting grace), but giveth grace unto the humble."*

And in 1 Pet 5:5 – 6 it's written, *"...for God resisteth the proud, and giveth grace to the humble. Humble yourselves therefore under the mighty hand of God, that he may exalt you in due time:"*

Word of knowledge:

"They whom do not reject the knowledge of God, will not be proud and full of their own boasts, for they shall recognize the call of the Spirit of grace and so their hearts shall be humbled unto the Lord and they shall be accepted of the Lord,"

For as Jesus touched the leper to be healed, so are the *humble* of heart healed through His grace and His truth through the effectual power of His Spirit, as they abide in Him.

A LACK OF KNOWLEDGE (TRUTH), is what makes men fall into the snares woven by the prince of this world (John 14:30) through false knowledge.

Truth and error, darkness and light, good and evil...this is contradictions. This is why men fall prey to the influence of the spirit of this world, of understanding scripture their own way and then creating false doctrines, lacking true discernment given of the Spirit of God, lacking a solid foundation (rock=Jesus Christ=altar) and form different denominations in an effort to seek and worship God their own way, for they walk in spiritual blindness, that is darkness, and darkness is because of ignorance about the truth of God through Jesus Christ our Lord. Also the Lord resists the proud and accepts the humble.

It's at this point of ignorance, that the ears are deaf and the eyes are blinded, for only the Spirit of grace can open the eyes to see (revelation of truth by grace) and unplug the ears to hear when truth is heard and accepted and the heart humbled, as the will of man yield to His grace, that calls all men from out of darkness unto the marvelous light of God and submit to the Spirit, that makes faith living.

When people refuse to hear or see, it's *rejecting* the gift of His grace by which we are saved through the truth of God, to walk contrary to God and not in submission to His Will.

Ephesians 2:5 says, *"Even when we were dead in sins, hath quickened us* (brought to life, from flesh to flame (spirit), from the old to the new man) *together with Christ (by grace ye are saved),"*

And in Ephesians 4:7 we read, *"But unto everyone of us* (those in covenant) *is given grace according to the measure of the gift of Christ* (truth, salvation)."

In Colossians 1: 5 – 6 we read,

"For the <u>hope</u> that is laid up for you in heaven, whereof ye heard before in the <u>word</u> <u>of the truth of the gospel</u>; Which is come unto you, as it is in all the world; and <u>bringeth forth</u> <u>fruit</u>, as it doth also <u>in</u> you, since the day ye heard of it, and <u>knew</u> the <u>grace of God</u> <u>in truth</u>:"

It's in the <u>ABSENCE</u> of truth that men do not know God through Jesus Christ; don't know what faith is; don't know how to worship God in righteousness; don't know how to abide in Him; don't know the works of the Spirit but do works of the flesh; that many truths evolve and each mouth testifies of a 'different' Jesus; its then that faith is in vain; that the soul reflects the fruits of iniquity and the conscience remains in condemnation; that the will is too weak to resist sin and the temptations of Satan's wiles; that the yoke of faith (Christ Jesus) is heavy and burdensome; that strife and contradiction rules in the body rather than the equity and peace of God and believers don't have the experience of true unity in the body being in one Spirit and in one truth.

When a person is trained through study in a profession of choice, and as an example, let's say someone qualifies as a medical doctor, that person will, after receiving his degree of qualification, be constantly drawing from that knowledge taught to him in the institution where he was accepted. His thoughts will be occupied mostly by thinking on procedures, medication, treatments, problems occurred and projecting on solutions drawing from the knowledge he acquired; after work he will most likely be talking work, sharing his experiences with either other medical orientated qualified people that would understand what he speaks about and in turn they will discuss medical issues, problems and solutions and share specific incidents regarding patients, occurred during the day as they analyze and mull over probable outcome or error; at home he will apply his training on those whom are in need of his expertise, he can hand out advise and be asked for advice by close relatives and friends.

The point being made, is that he is in all his ways, what he has been trained and qualified in. He thinks, talks and does his profession. The things he thinks, says and does, is who he is, it's who he has become by the knowledge he has been trained in. Can you see this?

Now apply this to being trained in knowledge that is either false (darkness) or truth (light). The very same thing, that was illustrated above, happens to man when being trained in the knowledge of this world on birth. We become the product of the knowledge we accept and work with, to express verbally the knowledge we have been trained in and so also are able to give physical expression of our 'expertise'. Can you see this? Man becomes the artwork/ finished product of false knowledge.

The knowledge we embrace (labor with) becomes the *affections* of the *heart* and is what we give utterance to. It is in this "affection" that we place our faith in. What proceeds from the mouth is an outward expression and testimony that clearly shows which kingdom we embrace and abide in. This is what defileth the soul, through the evil heart. What one consumes (partake of), one will outwardly express and this is the testimony that one lives (light) or die (darkness) by.

If the heart is evil, the reflection within is of darkness. For evil seeks only to increase by evil. Thus the imagination of man seeks only to profit himself in an acceptable way for the self, by man's own standard for life and faith, that *glorifies* himself and sets himself on a journey where *err and truth cannot be distinguished* in the absence of truth whilst in the presence of darkness.

The *evil heart* can only be cleansed from the fruits of evildoing within, by the process of *cleansing* by conformity to Jesus Christ's knowledge (truth), which is the *word* of God, as can be seen in Mark 1:40 – 42, Where a leper approached Jesus and beached Him to cleanse him from the leprosy of his flesh, *"if thou wilt, thou CANST make me clean"*...he acknowledged Jesus Christ as the Son of God by these words because it was given by the Father for Him to *see*, he expressed belief...he believed....no one told him to believe but he believed as it was given for him to *see* and acknowledged that he CAN be cleansed by the power of Jesus Christ if only he BELIEVED. Jesus reciprocated on his believing, *"And Jesus, moved with compassion, put forth his hand, and touched him, and saith unto him, I will; be thou clean"*

Here we can see the act of believing (faith) that brought healing through contact with Jesus Christ. He was healed because he could see Jesus Christ as the contact point for his faith in order for him to be healed. He responded in faith. He yielded to the power of Jesus by the Spirit of grace and humbled himself to Him, Jesus reciprocated on this act of faith expression and touched him, so by the power of Jesus the leper was healed. Jesus <u>spoke</u> and by His <u>words</u> this man was healed as His power was/is in His <u>word</u> <u>(truth).</u>

Therefore, By the *washing(cleansing)* of the truth of God as it penetrates the heart/soul, the heart is healed through contact with Jesus Christ in faith, for those who have eyes to see and ears to hear to become the new man in Christ... for the purifying of the heart is by faith. (Acts 15:9)

Therefore we can see that two things have to be present: *faith* in Christ and Him being the *contact point* for faith. There is an <u>exchange</u> taking place, faith's response to Jesus Christ as the Spirit bears witness of Him and Jesus reciprocating by His power to bring forth healing of the flesh, by the act of faith. Divine transformation by divine power.

Jesus said in John 7:18, "*He that speaketh OF himself seeketh his <u>own</u> glory...*" meaning that he that speaks from his *own* understanding, seeks to glorify himself. Which means interpreting/understanding His truth without the witness of the Spirit is to seek your own glory (pride, boast), because the Spirit will not give witness to what man perceives to be the truth.

It will not be a correct 'assumption' or analysis of scripture, as men then take scripture to a level of being a form of counseling (psychology) and an instrument that will reveal the will of God for ones life that only speaks of the self (what you want, what you need, resolving of issues) – meaning that what they come up with does not *confirm* Jesus Christ in truth.

Thus, when men discern *without* the power of the Spirit, their minds give understanding to what they *think* (imagination; using logic and reason with false knowledge) are meant (true), that always applies and points right back to the self.

IN CONCLUSION, it is important that believers understand, that they can't just believe what they want to belief, to be true about Jesus, but that they are to be led by the Spirit within the right environment (framework of truth) that will teach them all things pertaining to Jesus Christ in truth, being OF the Spirit as the solid foundation (knowledge=Jesus=altar=truth) is laid within under His stewardship. The reason for this is as follows: we already know there are two kingdoms at work and two powers and that both kingdoms require knowledge and the act of faith....believing.

When you believe, you acknowledge the knowledge presented, you mold with that knowledge and then you submit to the power that governs that kingdom. The spirit of the world (antichrist spirit) or the Spirit of God is the inspiration/power of each kingdom mentioned.

Believing is a process of submission by which the 'voice' of that kingdom becomes stronger, as we give it power of influence over us. Therefore we can also see that the act of faith, *to believe*, is a cognitive choice carried out by the believer, because it's done by your own free will.

So we can see that when we believe in Jesus, we are saying that we acknowledge Him as the Son of God, the truth of God and then we choose to mold with His knowledge and all things given for faith, as we yield our will unto the Lord to walk in His will and submit to the effectual working power of His Spirit.

Rom 10

"1. Brethren, my heart's desire and prayer to God for Israel is that they may be saved.

2. For I bear them a record that they have a zeal of God, but not according to knowledge.

3. For they, being ignorant of God's righteousness, and going about to establish their own righteousness, have not submitted themselves unto the righteousness of God.

4. For Christ is the end of the law or righteousness to everyone that believeth.

5. For Moses describeth the righteousness which is of the law, That the man that doeth those things shall live by them.

6. But the righteousness which is of faith speaketh of this wise, Say not in thy heart, Who shall ascend into heaven?(that is, to bring Christ down from above:)

7. Or who shall descend into the deep? (that is, to bring Christ again from the dead.)

8. But what saith it? The word is nigh thee, even in thy mouth, and in thy heart: that is, the word of faith, which we preach;

9. For if thou shalt confess with thy mouth the Lord Jesus, and thou shalt believe in thine heart that God hath raised him from the dead, thou shalt be saved.

10. For with the heart man believeth unto righteousness; and with the mouth confession is made unto salvation.

11. For the scripture saith, Whosoever believeth on him shall not be ashamed.

12. For there is no difference between the Jew and the Greek: for the same Lord over all is rich unto all that call upon him.

13. For whosoever shall call upon the name of the Lord shall be saved.

14. How then shall they call on him in whom they have not believed? and how shall they believe in him of whom they have not heard? and how shall they hear without a preacher?

15. And how shall they preach, except they be sent? as it is written, How beautiful are the feet of them that preach the gospel of peace, and bring glad tidings of good things!

16. But they have not all obeyed the gospel. For Esaias saith, Lord, who hath believed our report?

17. So then faith cometh by hearing, and hearing by the word of God.

18. But I say, Have they not heard? Yes, verily, their sound went into all the earth, and their words unto the ends of the world.

19. But I say, Did not Israel know? First Moses saith, I will provoke you to jealousy by them that are no people, and by a foolish nation I will anger you.

20. But Esias is very bold, and saith, I was found of them that sought me not; I was made manifest unto them that asked not after me.

21. But to Israel he said, "All day long I have stretched forth my hands unto a disobedient and gainsaying people."

May every man that heareth the word of God call upon Him and be saved according to the grace of the Lord, which calls all men unto Him to receive the hope of the gift of Christ.

Faith

Part 5

The tradition of Jesus Christ =The tradition of the true gospel of Jesus Christ

We open with Heb. 11.1 where we read,

"NOW FAITH is the SUBSTANCE of things HOPED for, the EVIDENCE of things not SEEN."

FAITH is to believe without seeing THAT which one believes in. Faith is a cognitive decision of the will to be humbled to God's will, as the Spirit of the Lord strengthens the will to walk in obedience to His will by grace and truth through faith. When one believe, one submit oneself into His care (in covenant) in order for God to teach one <u>all things</u> pertaining to His kingdom and the mystery He has hidden from the carnal mind, AND thus to form His Christ (fruit: virtue) within those whom yield to His grace that walk in <u>obedience</u> under His stewardship.

The HOPE of the righteous are in the promises of God that is set in Jesus Christ, who is the SUBSTANCE of that hope, so that we can inherit eternal life through Him when we accept God's terms and conditions and meet His expectation for true faith, that is to be re-educated in truth (knowledge of God), which results in conforming to His knowledge and labor with His spiritual tokens (contact points), through which we are purged, cleansed and healed from the scars inflicted upon our souls through contact with false knowledge and our thought patterns that reflectsSatan's likeness, through our first birth into this world, to take on the image and likeness of God through Jesus Christ, whilst remaining within His framework of truth.

The reality is (accepted or not) that Adamites have been deceived, blinded and lied to by the prince of the world (John 12:31), the master of deception, who has every intention to rob the heart of faith so that we will not be accepted by God.

We were taught to embrace Satan's knowledge within the knowledge system he designed, implemented and initiated for Adamites, to bring the judgments of God upon us because of disobedience. He has taught us to not value the things of God, by redirecting faith from Christ to the self. Thus from faith being "Christ-centered", to being "self=centered".

The EVIDENCE of "the substance of things hoped for" becomes the reality and new habit of faith (lifestyle), of the faithful, when they are enabled to OBSERVE God by the given tokens and knowledge and thus behold His face in all things given for faith by "Do-ing" righteousness. The evidence of their faith is the works they do, which are spiritual and the fruit born through that works is a testimony to the power of God to bring forth divine change within His divine power. The evidence of their transformation in MIND (renewing of the mind: Rom 12:2), is verbalized by the words they speak, which is charity (Col 3:14), the bond of perfectness, by which a multitude of sins are covered. Charity is the spiritual sacrifices (prophesy) reciprocated unto God, which is well pleasing to Him as it reflects the only gift He finds acceptable, His Christ Jesus. Charity is the words spoken, that is the knowledge of Jesus Christ = Truth = doctrine => knowledge of God being reciprocated unto Him as a gift that is equal to Himself, that is seen as the expression of faith, as they keep His commandments. The words they speak bear witness to the changed perspective formed within the mind, through the process of regeneration, through their activity of faith by partaking of Jesus. Those of faith, BELIEVE in the invisible, but the invisible is in fact the true reality, that has been hidden from man's eyes for the heart to be tested when grace comes knocking on the door of the heart.

On conversion (Luke 22: 31), the Spirit bears witness to the record of faith (Jesus Christ), so that the eyes behold the invisible God by grace and truth.

Faith is the LIFESTYLE of the righteous doing works of the Spirit, that establishes Jesus Christ as the affection of the heart (focus point), as all idols of the heart are laid before the altar and He is placed upon the throne of the heart.

The following scripture was brought to mind, Matt 8:10, about the centurion who came to Jesus in Capernaum, to beseech Him to heal his very sick servant of the palsy. He told Jesus that He could only speak the word and he shall be healed. Jesus said in verse 10, *"Verily I say unto you, I have not found so great faith, no not in Israel."* This man being not of Israel, believed in Jesus Christ, and believed that He could heal by the AUTHORITY of His WORD only. He expressed faith without seeing the evidence of what he believed in and Jesus was amongst the chosen nation of faith, that did not express that same faith, for He said, *"I have not found so great faith, no not in Israel."* On his belief, Jesus said to him, *"Go thy way; and as thou hast believed, so it be done unto thee."* and his servant was healed. He believed.

Did you know that there are 3 manifestations of faith?

1. Faith, doctrine. Which is the knowledge (truth) of Jesus Christ, which is all facts consistent to God's character, purpose and plan.
2. Faith, the fruit. This is the increase of the soul with the temperament of Jesus Christ which is the virtue of the Spirit. 3. Faith, the gift. This is the empowerment of the will by the Spirit, to remain obedient to God in the most trying and adverse of situations.

Let's look at this for a moment:

1. The doctrine (truth) persuades us of our faith in Jesus Christ and is consistent with what was given to the apostles by Jesus, therefore no altering of His truth. It is pure and wholesome doctrine that is the knowledge of God.

In Timothy 1:4 we read *"Neither give heed to fables and endless genealogies* [doctrines of men, cause spiritual drunkenness], *which minister questions* [doubt, double mindedness], *rather than godly edifying* [truth] <u>*which is of faith*</u>*: so do."* The <u>doctrine of faith</u> unites all that call upon the Lord, and partakes of Him in His covenant, in unfeigned faith (Tim 1:5) and spiritual unity with charity as the expression of Christ (truth), that is the expression of God's love. Thus, Charity is the verbal expression of the doctrine of God which is the expression of Jesus by the lips of the righteous. The doctrines of men lead to drunkenness, which means the mind is intoxicated with the substance of false knowledge that makes the eyes and ears dull, to not see the light but to walk in darkness (ignorance).

In 1 Tim 6: 3 we read, *"If any man teach otherwise* (other than truth, thus false knowledge, doctrines of men*), and consent not* (protestors stand in opposition and in doubt, double mindedness and sedition / grace resisters =sinners / opposing stewardship*) to wholesome words* (stewardship*), even the words of our Lord Jesus Christ, and to the doctrine* (truth) *which is according to godliness* (from Above); *He is proud, knowing nothing, but doting about questions and strife of words, whereof cometh envy, strife, railings, evil surmisings, perverse disputings of men of corrupt minds* (false knowledge corrupts the mind and scars the soul*), and destitute of the truth (*faith is in vain), *supposing that gain is godliness* (feigned by will): *from such withdraw thyself."*

The spirit of this world would not have man be <u>content</u> <u>in</u> <u>God</u>, but rather be <u>discontent</u>. To be "content in God" means to be in "equity with God", this speaks of our <u>union with God</u>.

The ungodly are discontent and seek resolve for outcome by their own power and counsel, standing independent from God, making Him subject to man. To gain the world, the ungodly and discontent, is unprofitable (decrease of soul/ building for the self rather than for God) in the kingdom of God.

But the godly are content in God, stand in agreement with the knowledge taught, conform to it, being in one mind and one perspective as co-labourers of Christ Jesus. Therefore the apostle said, *"But godliness with contentment is great gain."*(1 Timothy 6:6)

To be CONTENT in God means to have faith (to believe) in the work God does within the soul through Jesus Christ and therefore walking after the rhythm of the Spirit of truth.

Furthermore, we read in 1 Tim 6:10 + 21, *"For the love of money is the root of all evil: which while some coveted after, they have <u>erred from the faith</u> (truth), and pierced themselves through with many sorrows. (21) Which some professing have erred concerning the faith..."*

We cannot serve two masters, either one or the other. We cannot eat from two tables, thus saying we cannot partake of the world (mammon) and God, for the one will be served well and the other neglected, and the inspiration (power) of the kingdom we <u>give ear</u> too, is the kingdom we serve through the knowledge we embrace, whose 'voice' becomes stronger as it molds the perspective of the mind into the likeness of the master of that kingdom, as we conform to the knowledge we choose to embrace; for anything that is NOT truth is not OF God and thus if man follows after that, he serves the master of this world, who is the prince of this world, whose spirit rules this atmosphere. The love (speaking of when one's expectation is set in self advancement - building - for the self, by the self, through the self) for this life (world: lust of the eyes/lust of the flesh/pride of life), brings ruin (death) to the soul. But he who despises (turn away) this life (flesh) and accepts death (death in Christ Jesus) willingly in submission to God's will, he shall live (resurrected with Christ Jesus) eternally (inherit the promises of God through Jesus).

We cannot profess Jesus in faith but reject Him in covenant, for then we err from the faith of righteousness.

Rom 1:5, *"By whom we have received grace and apostleship, for obedience to the faith"*

1 John 2:15. *"Love not the world, neither the things that are in the world. If any man loves the world, the love of the Father is not in him."*

2. The fruit of faith is that which is born (increase) within the soul that reflects the work God is doing within the soul through contact with the tokens of the Spirit, through faith's labor. This speaks of the lifestyle of the righteous that testify to the change within (new man) from that which is of the flesh, to that which is of the Spirit (new man). For they walk by faith and not by sight. The fruits of faith are the fruits of the Spirit by which they are found acceptable by the Lord.

It is not only fruit unto virtue that is born within, but a love for God by His standard (not speaking of emotional love) within the heart and mind (being placed on the throne of the heart/ closing the door of the imagination and reflecting on Jesus' knowledge), as trust in the Lord is strengthened through the evidence of His work within the soul manifested in times of testing, when the response to offense and contradiction has changed, for now the mind labor with truth rather than accepting the lure of the flesh presented to the mind, as the track well used. Thus all thoughts are taken captive in Christ and placed on the scale of truth, weighed and a choice of faith is made, to accept the inclination of man or to die to the self, the world and Satan.

1 Tim 1:19 says, *"Holding faith, and a good conscience: which some having put away concerning faith have made shipwreck:"*

Jesus Christ stands in the door of the conscience when grace and truth is present in faith's labor (covenant), for as He is pure and undefiled, so is the conscience of the righteous. For the conscience reflects the giver of knowledge, unto death or unto life. And thus, so it's written, *"Fight the good fight of faith, lay hold on eternal life, whereunto thou art also called, and hast professed a good profession before many witnesses."* 1 Timothy 6:12

3. The gift of faith, is a spiritual gift issued, as the Spirit wills, to sustain the soul through which the soul is enabled to withstand even the severest of testing, through the issuance of a measure of grace to strengthen the will to remain obedient to the will of God during these times.

We read in Heb 11:33 -35, how the patriarchs before and others named also (ex: the prophets, Samson, Gedeon, Barak, king David), stood steadfast in faith doing the will of God, seeking not resolve and outcome from circumstance but through faith persevered and was strengthened by grace to stand in His promises, walking in cadence with the Lord.

Thus by the gift of faith, the righteous stand strong through obedience in faith, sustained by the grace of God, for grace lacketh naught.

In Rom.12:3 we read, *"For I say, through the grace given unto me,to every man that is among you, not to think of himself more highly than he ought to think; but to think <u>soberly</u>, according as God has dealt to every man <u>the measure of faith.</u>"*

Faith pleases God. Faith that follows the pattern for life as given through Jesus Christ (Heb 8:5 – 6/ 1 Tim 1: 16), who is the record for faith in which all things is set (wholesome knowledge, tokens, terms of the covenant) for the transformation of the soul to be accepted by God. For those of faith in covenant with God, meet the expectation of God for the soul to return unto perfection in order for them to abide in His Light eternally.

"And having a high priest [Jesus Christ] over the house of God; Let us draw near with a true heart in full assurance of faith, having our hearts sprinkled from an evil conscience, and our bodies washed with pure water.

Let us hold fast the profession of our faith without wavering; (for he is faithful that promised;)" Heb 10: 21 - 23

Faith

Part 6

The tradition of Jesus Christ =The tradition of the true gospel of Jesus Christ

Works of faith through Spiritual contact points:

The word "works" does not imply that we "earn" our redemption. This is a misconception pertaining to faith that is commonly thought of and accepted by many believers today.

We cannot appease or please God or earn our redemption by doing works of the flesh outside of His covenant restrictions, using our talents and gifts received from the Lord, as these things were not given by God for faith's activity (works). The Spirit won't quickeneth faith that is built on the shifting foundations of the flesh. Our signature gifts and talents are given for the sole purpose of living our lives in this world, for our pleasure (expression of the self) and for the purpose of making a living, if you so wish.

Believers should not confuse these with spiritual contact points that beget works of the Spirit.

Salvation is free, but it's not free from responsibility:

Thus saying, salvation came by Jesus Christ and is freely given unto all men that call upon the name of the Lord, but God has His conditions and terms for salvation to be effective, and for faith to be accepted by Him.

God designed faith with our participation in mind within a framework (restrictions) of truth with the "things" (tokens/spiritual contact points) He designed and sprinkled with the blood of Christ, within a spiritual priesthood, that all have to enter into to be partakers of Christ and joint-heirs to the Throne of glory and power.

By these tokens we are joined to God to be partakers of Christ.

In Rom 14: 17 -18 we read, *"For the kingdom of God is not in meat and drink, but in the righteousness, and peace, and joy in the Holy Ghost.*

For he that in <u>these things</u> serveth Christ is acceptable to God, and approved of men."

In Phil 2:12 we read, "... work out your own salvation with fear and trembling." The choice remains ours, whether we accept the gift of grace and submit to the Spirit of truth, which works a good work within the consenters of His plan and it is then their (consenters) responsibility to function within the framework of truth by being obedient through faith; the righteous according to God's standard, enter through the veil to behold the kingdom of God in all its power and glory through obedience to His terms as they function in their priesthood.

Therefore, lets recap: These "things" that the apostle Paul referred to, are the spiritual contact points provided by God, that He has given, for us to be <u>joined</u> to Him, for the spiritual transformation of the soul by being partakers (touching Him) of Jesus Christ by partaking of the grace and truth that God has set in these things, to give us a real and living experience of faith and for the process of regeneration to worketh the new man in Christ Jesus. For the power of grace and truth is within each one of these contact points. Very much like these "touch lights" one place in a child's room; the moment one places one's hand on it, it lights up, "touching" releasing the energy to bring forth light. So too is it with these spiritual contact points, the moment we touch them in faith, through faith's labor (activity), the same moment God's grace and truth is released, to impact the soul.

God designed salvation so that He could come in contact with the soul and so affect a divine change within, which would form the soul in the image of Jesus. God wants to come in contact with the soul in an environment that is set apart (separated from the world) and fruitful for faith.

Phil 1:6, *"Being confident of this very thing, that he which hath <u>begun a good work</u> in you will perform it until the day of Jesus Christ:"*

It was for this reason that God came in the flesh as Jesus Christ, to die and be resurrected: for His death was for our release from the penalty of sin and His resurrection for our release from the power of sin.

Rom 5:10, *"For if, when we were enemies, we were <u>reconciled</u> to God by the <u>death</u> of his Son, much more, being reconciled, we shall be saved by his <u>life</u>."*

The soul needs interaction and the reality of faith, in order for it to be changed. We cannot have faith in God through our imagination, for there is no power in it and no real interaction, nor any divine change that takes place. So, Jesus provided us with the means of partaking of Him when He died and rose from death, for our faith to be a living reality.

In 1 Cor.6:17 we read, "But he that is joined unto the Lord is ONE Spirit." The word "joined" refers to a point of contact, a point of access that joins us to God and God to us.

And in Rom.5:2 we read, "By whom (Jesus) also we have access by faith into this grace wherein we stand, and rejoice in hope of the glory of God." Our access to God is Jesus Christ, the door through which we have to enter (step) in order to be partakers of God's grace and truth. (Jn.10:9).

When Jesus ascended to heaven, He sent us the Holy Spirit, to provide us with the reality of a living faith. Through our contact with the Holy Spirit, we partake of Jesus and the contact points He (God) provided for our <u>joining</u> to Him.

We are allowed to touch (partake) God by our contact with the Holy Spirit, thus partaking of the power of His grace and truth that He has set in each one of His spiritual contact points, to effect a divine change within the soul.

Eph.3:6, "That the Gentiles should be fellow-heirs, and of the same body and partakers of His promise in Christ by the gospel."

God promised us communion with Him (through the Holy Spirit), forgiveness of our sins and remission of sins, which means the healing of the soul from the effects of iniquity. But God is a Spirit and our communion with Him has to be on the same grounds to be of any effect and to thus give us the experience of a living faith, therefore He provided these contact points by which our faith are quickened by the effectual working power of the Holy Spirit. It's by these things that we come to know Him, fellowship/communicate with Him and experience His work within us. We cannot partake of Him with fleshly things, as He is a Spirit, as Jesus was in the flesh, but now He is a Spirit too.

2 Cor 5:16 say, *"...yea, though we have known Christ after the flesh, yet now henceforth know we him no more."*

Let's recap on this: It stands to reason, that if His power is in each one of these things, then in <u>touching</u> it (partaking of it), the power set inside it, will be <u>released</u> to effect change within the inner man. Partaking of it, requires an activity, and it is by this activity that transformation takes place within the soul, as grace gains an access point to the soul by yielding of the will to His grace. Can you see that?

In 2 Pet.1:3-4 we read, *"According <u>as his divine power</u> has given to us all <u>things</u> that pertain unto life and godliness, through the knowledge of Him that has called us to glory and virtue:"* Through our access to God the soul is divinely transformed and takes on the form of godliness, as we bear the fruits of that contact which is called virtue.

Reading 2 Cor 5:17, When the old is replaced with the new, a divine change within takes place (new man) IF we are IN Christ, rooted in His knowledge and partaking of Him through our contact with His spiritual contact points for faith, for says he, *"old things are passed away; behold, all things are become new."*

It therefore speaks of: The <u>physical (old)</u> is replaced by the <u>spiritual (new)</u>, the Law and its physical contact points as given to Moses, has passed away and now "all things", all the contact points, is now spiritual, for Jesus came to establish a spiritual covenant where we are joined to Him and His Father as ONE through access to the Holy Spirit that quickens our faith. The glory of the new supersedes the glory of the old.

Therefore, we have access to God through Jesus Christ, as Jesus provided these things in Himself because He is our access to God and our communion with Him.

God has given to us spiritual things, which enable us to partake of Jesus Christ, to touch Him, not just remember Him. The remembrance is meant to be a living memorial of His death and resurrection, which the Spirit quickens. That is why we call these spiritual things "contact points". This is what the first apostles taught and is what the Bible teaches as well.

We see that the effect of Christ upon the soul is through grace (Jas.4:6) and truth (Jn.1:17) and that truth takes the form of doctrine.

Our Will is humbled by the grace that is made manifest through these contact points, that was given to the body through the stewardship of the apostles of old, as given by Jesus for the communion of the body with God through Him.

The spiritual contact points are those things the righteous in Jesus, remaining within the restrictions of faith, partake of (touch) through their labor of faith, that has been lost to the church, and is thus that which was given unto them by God to partake of the fullness of Christ unto completion of the soul: prayer, prophesy, preaching, the gifts of the spirit, graces of God (manifestation of dreams, visions), callings, truth, the Spirit and His government through which He stewards His grace and truth. These things join us to Him, and it is a point of access for His grace to effect change within and strengthen the will to remain consistent in following the pattern of faith as given through Jesus Christ. These are the things believers handle, in order to touch Christ partaking of Him, to be joined to God, and thus receive the glory of the Lord, as His glory (virtue) is manifested in the soul.

We are only in the kingdom of Light when we abide (partake) in Jesus, and do righteousness, which means serving Him in word and in deed and not in word only.

In John 4:24, the apostle John said, *"God is a Spirit: and they that worship Him must worship Him in spirit and in truth"*

The things of the Spirit can only be spiritually discerned by those who have the common faith in Jesus Christ.

The Spirit of God will not give witness to anything of man that is by his own reason and logic (own discernment), through which he reserves the right to discern the truth of God and exalt himself above the witness of the Spirit.

For did Jesus not say in John 6:63 *"....the words that I speak unto you, they are spirit, and they are life."*?

The words He *spoke* was His *truth*, the words He spoke gives *life* and *is life*, for as much did He not also say *"I am the way, the truth and the life..."* (John 14:6)

Life comes through Jesus Christ; He, the Father and the Spirit are ONE (John 14:11) therefore He is also Spirit and by His Spirit life is given unto those who believeth in His words.

In John 14:17, Jesus said, *"Even the spirit of truth; whom the world cannot receive, because it sees him not, neither knoweth him: but ye know him; for he dwelleth with you, and shall be in you."*

Jesus is the truth witnessed by the *Spirit of truth*, who cannot be seen without the revelation of the Father who is Spirit that bear witness to Jesus.

It's plainly said that when the world is not able to see Him, they will not KNOW Him and therefore will not recognise Him. We can only see Jesus and thus God, if we are of the Spirit. (John 14:7/ John 14:9). Seeing God through Jesus speaks of observing the face of Jesus in His truth as the Spirit bears witness to Jesus Christ. When we see Jesus, we see God, by knowing Jesus. We know Jesus when we abide in Him and follow His commandments.

In Math 16:13 Jesus asked His disciples *"Whom do men say I the Son of man am?"* From their answer in verse 14, it's clear that many people did not see (recognise) Him as the Son of God, they could not SEE Him as it was not revealed by the father unto them that He WAS the Messiah all have been waiting for, but then Jesus asked them, *"But whom say ye that I am?"*(vers15)

From the response of Simon Peter, *"Thou art the Christ, the Son of the living God"*, Jesus reveals one very important thing by saying (verse 17)*"... blessed art thou Simon Bar-jona: for flesh and blood hath not revealed it unto thee, but my Father which is in heaven"* and thus it is, that the revelation of Christ is by the Spirit of God only. Only by the will of God can those behold the face of Jesus in all things, when called by God and they reciprocate in faith unto righteousness.

Furthermore Jesus said in the same verse: "but he that seeketh his (Gods) glory that sent him (Jesus), the same is true, and no unrighteousness is IN him." Meaning, that he who seeks the Lord out of a pure heart shall see the glory of the Lord, for His glory is within them. As His Spirit teaches them all things.

How is the truth taken into different directions?

*By Interpretation of scripture, in the absence of the Holy Spirit outside the boundaries God has set for faith's expression and our experience of faith.

*By taking scripture and making it applicable to one's own life, as though God is revealing His will for your life/circumstances/needs/struggles.

*By not remaining within the sanctified environment of His covenant restrictions, in order for faith to remain centered on Jesus Christ and the knowledge (doctrine) to remain pure, untouched and unchanged by the minds (imagination) of men that follow the course of their own passions and principles based on what they belief to be true, in denominational churches/belief systems, by which Jesus Christ is subject to the passions of man and not man being subject to God through Jesus Christ.

We were created for the good pleasure of God, and not God for ours.

Therefore we now know:

The Holy Spirit is the one that bears witness to Jesus Christ. (John 5:32, 37) It's through the Holy Spirit that understanding is gained about the truth. Understanding comes through the witness, the witness of the Holy Spirit. The witness confirms Jesus Christ as the record for our faith.

By the witness of the Spirit we are able to know Jesus Christ. (Math 16:17) (John 6:67)

The Spirit of God alone bears witness of Jesus Christ (John 5: 32, 37; John 8:18) in His covenant that He came to establish in Himself as the record of our faith (John 8:14), so if the knowledge is not pure and have been changed (misrepresented), then it's not reflecting Jesus and therefore the Holy Spirit will not bear witness to it.

When the Spirit of God is not the witness, then it's a surety that another spirit is at work with this knowledge in order for a believer to "believe" this altered knowledge, that sets the believer on a journey away from God although they think it's in line with God's truth.

The spirit of this world will not bring believers into God's care, but will keep them on endless unfruitful journeys whereby they are still daily in doubt of salvation, remission of sins and struggle with their inability to not do sin or keep them under a delusion that they are walking in faith with God, through their experiences received by this worldly spirit.

Preaching this chiseled knowledge, AS the doctrine of Jesus Christ by a spirit that is not of God misleads and redirects faith from Jesus to the self. Although it might feel right, sound right and is received by those who hunger for truth as right, it's not the truth of Christ Jesus when altered to fit the passions of a man. This is done through ignorance, because the path of righteousness is observed and followed through by the power of the Spirit of God, who is the witness of Jesus Christ that bears witness to Him as being the Son of God and through whose power the face of Jesus can be seen in the truth taught.

This is also true about the meaning of the word "faith".

If a believer does not know what faith is, how to express faith, how to practice faith(DO) and thus walk in the perfect will of God (which is Jesus Christ expressed in and through faiths activity for the new man to be born in and through Christ Jesus), then they consider "believing" is enough by confession of faith, which is that they believe that Jesus Christ is the Son of God, that He died on the cross and was resurrected on the 3rd day, that He died for the sins of the world and that through Him all who believe is saved.

"Believing" alone is not enough, faith needs the right knowledge and an activity to take place within the right environment, with the right contact points, to set in motion the transformation of the soul and the re-education of the mind, called spiritual cleansing from false- to true knowledge, to be true faith as by God's standard.

We can see today, how division and strife has entered amongst believers that have set each one on a different path (denominations), but all say they worship ONE God.

In James 3:14 – 16 we read, *"But if ye have bitter envying and strife in your hearts, glory not, And lie not against the truth. This wisdom* (wisdom of the world) *descendeth not from above, but is earthly* (flesh), *sensual* (lust of man), *devilish* (contrary to God). *For where envying and strife* (inequity) *is, there is confusion and evil work* (false knowledge, traditions of men)."

Satan the deceiver is the author of lies that begets confusion that begets envy, strife, emulations and diversities.

By cleverly dividing believers into many different belief systems, albeit many believe in ONE God through Jesus Christ, and others not

- there is no unity in doctrine (truth) taught, due to everyone applying it in the way they understand it:
- Private interpretation follows the way of will worship ...taking verses or parts of the scripture, interpreting it according to one's own needs and circumstance and then applying it to one's own life, saying that it is the will of God for one's own life. This is not true.

The will of God speaks not of what's good for your life, what will make you happy, what will make you financially stable, what will give you a better future or a happy relationship (marriage/friendship etc).

The will of God is Jesus Christ.

Satan has taught man to doubt and distrust God, to seek his own counsel, to walk in his own strength, to seek his own peace and security by adjusting his circumstances through his own measure and enforcing his own principles on others, so that the balance could be corrected.

How can believers worship God in many different ways, when He says, "I AM the way, the truth and the life:" (John 14:6)

He says, "I AM THE way."

Meaning He will show the right path to walk on, through Jesus Christ, as Jesus came before us, to set the path before us. When he leads, those in truth, walk in His counsel and light. THEN they are in right standing with God.

Thus, God has provided the way for all that belief in Him to follow. This way is not your way, my way or her way, but Gods way.

The way of His Covenant faith, that Jesus Himself came to establish on earth and that came in effect on His death and resurrection.

His way follows faith expression in WORD (truth =doctrine) and in DEED (activity).

When believers give each unto his own understanding, interpretation of scripture and self determine the meaning of the word "faith" each according to his own understanding there is confusion, there is division in the absence of true UNITY of the Spirit and stewardship, for they are not in one mind and in one accord, nor in one faith and one spirit.

If all is not in one mind, one truth and in one faith, then there shall be confusion present and many diverse ways of understanding the way and the truth of the Lord, because His way IS restricted to what He finds acceptable, not man. His way IS spiritual and NOT carnal; His way brings UNITY amongst believers as they are united in ONE Spirit, ONE Truth and in ONE mind, being in agreement with God (equity) on His plan for salvation through Jesus Christ.

God is not a God of division or diversities, for His truth (doctrine) is Jesus Christ and His Truth is the sanctified (set apart) system that He gave to believers through His chosen Apostles that taught believers how to walk in covenant with Him (in righteousness) and how to worship God the way God wanted them to worship Him (acceptable way), and be free of the bondage of sin and death and the fruits thereof as they experience remission of sins daily due to them walking in truth according to the specifications He gave for this expression of faith. Through Jesus Christ man was reconciled to God, to be AT peace with God and to have

THE peace of God within their hearts through the way they worshiped God, given to them by those He appointed for this specific purpose. In the time of the Apostles, believers abided in ONE doctrine (truth), were in ONE mind and thus in ONE faith, as the Spirit of God made their faith a living experience.

THIS is then the manifestation of faith. They believe in the same thing, are in the same mind of what is being taught and are bound together by the bonds of charity, the love of God, as trust/ conviction is born within the heart.

The word "faith" is randomly and thoughtlessly used in everyday conversations, that does not confirm/testify Jesus Christ and His redemptive power by the Holy Spirit, but tells us about where one is placing one's own confidence and trust in, that is something else than Jesus Christ.

Saying the word "faith" doesn't make a person a believer, nor does it make one a faithful servant of the Lord, nor does using the word "faith" express Jesus Christ or make the user of that word a righteous, justified, sanctified holy person. For this to happen, work is needed, that is not of this world, but is of God through Jesus Christ.

Faith is all about Jesus Christ. Faith reflects Christ, confirms Christ and expresses Christ, as the Only Sacrifice that was and is acceptable to God for the redemption and salvation of man through an activity that has to take place for this faith to be of profit to the soul.

In James 1 - 3, faith and the importance of works is continually highlighted, for so it's written that faith without works is in vain, its dead faith.

In JAMES 2: 26 we read, *"For as the body without the spirit is dead, so faith without works is dead also"*

It's the works through faith's expression that defines the value and acceptability of faith before God.

Today the religious denominational churches follow the perception that the "works" spoken of, refers to physical works done (works of the flesh) by believers to express their faith, their love to God and thus by this standard they honor Him and abide in Him and they are in expectation that God will be very pleased and appeased by this show of works and so bless them with things by which they and everyone else, will know that His favor is upon them and that He finds their faith acceptable.

But this is a false mindset and a form of exploiting Jesus Christ for one's own benefit. For the works spoken of is not that which is done through physical activities in churches, like feeding the poor, taking care of the needy, random or orchestrated expressions of kindness to the destitute or less fortunate. These things have no effect (does not profit) on faith and thus cannot increase the kingdom of God, it cannot strengthen, increase or empower your faith, it cannot bring anyone into the fullness of Christ and it doesn't please God because nothing of Christ is IN that activity taking place.

However, it IS an expression of the nature of God, that he has set within each soul He has created to be kind and good. But it's not to be used to express faith with and neither to be called "faith".

Faith

Part 7

We begin with words received. And led by the Spirit, I went to Isaiah 43, where the Lord spoke through the prophet, confirming the words received below.

"Let them who have ears, hear and let them who have eyes, see, for so sayeth the Lord their God: Be unto me a holy nation, an undefiled and perfect nation, in whom I have great pleasure, for by My works thou shalt be set free and become like the Son of Man, for in His image am I who made ye. Everlasting am I; the son of perdition has no hold on the Son of Man; for thou shalt sit on the right hand of My throne in the coming of the Lord. Woe unto them who heed not the words of the Lord, for He speaks now of the life of fire and light in whom is the promises fulfilled unto everlasting peace. Peace be unto those who see the face of the Lord, for they shall be the heirs of His Throne."

"The tribe of the Lord is the tribe of His portion, the true Israelites of faith. For its not by the blood that flows in the veins of the Israelite nation, chosen to be the portion of the Lord, that make them faithful servants of the Lord by their faith, but by the Blood that has bought them free from bondage unto sin, to walk in the liberty of Jesus Christ, freed from the wiles of Satan, to be by faith, approved of the Lord." [Words received by the inspiration of the Spirit.]

And the word of the Lord spake through the prophet Isaiah (43: 7-), thus saying:

"Even every one that is called by my name: for I have created him for my glory, I have formed him; yea, I have made him.

Bring forth the blind people that have eyes, and the deaf that have ears.

Let all the nations be gathered together, and let the people be assembled: who among them can declare this, and show us former things? Let them bring forth their witnesses, that they be justified: or let them hear, and say, it is truth.

Ye are my witnesses, saith the Lord, and my servant whom I have chosen: that ye may know and believe me, and understand that I am he: before me there was no God formed, neither shall there be after me.

I, even I, am the Lord, and beside me there is no savior.

I have declared, and have saved, and I have shown, when there was no strange god among you: therefore ye are my witnesses, saith the Lord, that I am God.

Yea, before the day was I am he; and there is none that can deliver out of my hand: I will work, and who shall let it?

Thus saith the Lord, your redeemer, the Holy One of Israel; For your sake I have sent to Babylon, and have brought down all their nobles, and the Chaldeans, whose cry is in the ships.

I am the Lord, your Holy One, the creator of Israel, your King. Thus saith the Lord, which maketh a way in the sea, and a path in the mighty waters;

Which bringeth forth the chariot and horse, the army and the power; they shall lie down together, they shall not rise: they are extinct, they are quenched as two.

Remember ye not the former things, neither consider the things of old. Behold, I will do a NEW THING: now it shall spring forth; shall ye not know it? I will even make a way in the wilderness, and rivers in the desert, to give drink to my people, my chosen.

These people have I formed for myself; they shall show forth my praise.

Micah 4: 1-5 (KJV)

4 But in the last days it shall come to pass, that the mountain of the house of the LORD shall be established in the top of the mountains, and it shall be exalted above the hills; and people shall flow unto it.

2 And many nations shall come, and say, Come, and let us go up to the mountain of the LORD, and to the house of the God of Jacob; and he will teach us of his ways, and we will walk in his paths: for the law shall go forth of Zion, and the word of the Lord from Jerusalem.

3 And he shall judge among many people, and rebuke strong nations afar off; and they shall beat their swords into plowshares, and their spears into pruning hooks: nation shall not lift up a sword against nation, neither shall they learn war any more. 4 But they shall sit every man under his vine and under his fig tree; and none shall make them afraid: for the mouth of the Lord of hosts hath spoken it.

5 For all people will walk every one in the name of his god, and we will walk in the name of the Lord our God for ever and ever.

The following came to mind:

.In the last days, the House of the Lord shall be raised up, as He calls them by grace and they call upon the name of the Lord, their God. Thus the saints of the Lord partake of His substance and increase the kingdom of the Lord by faith through fruit-bearing unto virtue, being pillars in the House of the Lord.

For on the Mountain the House of God is seen from afar and all desire to live in it, but few are willing to climb the long and winding road to the top of that mountain.

Jacob became Israel, the father of the 12 tribes chosen by God to enter into the Promised Land under stewardship of Moses, by which the law given by God was taught unto the Israelites, the chosen and beloved of God.

The true Israelites are those of faith, not by birth but by faith, being the seed of Abraham, unto whom righteousness was imputed because he believed and followed God in all His ways.

For as much as those called Israelites by birth was the portion of the Lord, the Lord God provoked them to jealousy and gave their inheritance to those who sought Him not and knew Him not, the gentiles, due to the turning away of their hearts from the covenant God made with them.

Believers know their hope of salvation is in Jesus, but even though we have attained that hope, by the Blood of Jesus, we are responsible towards God, to seek Him in due diligence and remain within His restrictions for faith to be made perfect in and through Jesus Christ, so that we can enter into His promises made. We must remember that the promise of salvation through Jesus is for all the world, as God calls all unto Him, but a few are chosen, for not all men have faith. Entrance into the Promised land, is for the chosen, beloved and obedient tribe of Israel, that walk not by sight, but by faith.

Revelations is the last book in the Bible, and for many a book they try to avoid as long as possible. I've heard many believers confess that they fear to read it, it scares them, and many say they have no idea what it's all about, all the symbolisms used in it, confuses the mind, and therefore they avoid it, because their understanding is in part, as their faith is in part, for when faith is in part, there can be no discernment. For if there was discernment by inspiration of the Spirit, it would be revealed to be a book of pure prophecy, that would have placed many a believer on a journey to seek the Lord diligently and consistently.

The Book of Revelations, is a book of prophecy, to be used by the appointed Stewards of God's Covenant in this time, as it addresses the condition of the church, the doctrine and the future of the church.

God used many symbols to illustrate the points He was addressing through revelation to the Apostle John, for the church to stay on the tracks of truth and to exhort and edify them (Church) in remaining strong through faith and running a good race to the finish line.

In Revelations 22:18 – 21, Apostle John is the witness of the sayings of the Book of revelations, given to him to bring to the ears of men.

In verse 19, the word "take away" stood out, and brought to remembrance that this did not refer to a literal act of removing words from scripture/text, although it is now common practise to do so or to change the words or add another more modern word that would fit in with the generation of the time when the Bible is reprinted.

No, "take away" means to "remove", to remove something/someone from a specific place/position temporarily or permanently.

So, what can man "take away" from the prophecy of this book then?

When man brings the things of God's kingdom down to the level of his own carnal understanding and then uses private interpretation to complete his perceived concept of what he understands to be true.

Then, we 'remove' God(subject to man) from His rightful place to take His place. We cannot understand the truth by the carnal mind that worketh with false knowledge, inspired by the antichrist spirit.

Also, there are promises unto those who do 'take away" from the book of prophecy, a righteous judgment from the Lord.

Revelation 22:18-21 King James Version (KJV)

18 For I testify unto every man that heareth the words of the prophecy of this book, If any man shall add unto these things, God shall add unto him the plagues that are written in this book: 19 And if any man shall <u>take away</u> from the words of the book of this prophecy, God shall take away his part out of the book of life, and out of the holy city, and from the things which are written in this book.

20 He who testifieth these things saith, Surely I come quickly.

Amen. Even so, come, Lord Jesus.

21 The grace of our Lord Jesus Christ be with you all. Amen.

What Baptism do we need for salvation?

That of water, or that of the Spirit?

Reading Eph. 4:4-5 the following is said: "There is one body, and one Spirit, even as you are called in one hope of your calling. One Lord, one faith, ONE BAPTISM"

Clearly it is written "ONE Lord, ONE faith, ONE Baptism."

This refers to the Baptism of the Spirit which is needed and associated for entrance into Covenant with God, the New and Better Covenant, that is SPIRITUAL and not PHYSICAL.

Great discontent, strife and division rules amongst believers (the Church) today, on this very important activity that must take place. *Repentance and a confession of faith* are intended to be sealed with the *Baptism of the Spirit.*

Confusion in the church regarding the place value of *water baptism* and the *Baptism of the Spirit*, is due to the *lack of understanding* through *spiritual discernment* in the church, about both these two baptisms (their value) and the purpose for each one as by the Intent of God, who is the Designer, Initiator and Implementer of the *Pattern and Record for faith*, within the *Standard* (Jesus) that He has set for our salvation.

Transgressions of the church against God, being independent from God, by following the traditions of men, is due to the lack *of proper stewardship* that came through the Apostles office, those of the Spirit called by grace to fulfill that specific purpose, to be the eyes of the church.

Relating it to a physical body, the "eye" sees, and directs the body to walk in a way where no harm will befall it. So too, were the eyes of the church, the ordained apostles.

Can you see this?

If the eye is blinded, the body will fall by stumbling over that which is in its way or step into a hole the eye couldn't see, even unto death or the body through direction of the eyes, could negotiate its way around the stumbling blocks and around the holes to walk in safety, although there is some effort implied in doing this.

Jesus Christ was baptized by John to carry the sins of the Old

Testament people to the cross so their sins could be forgiven

Reading in Matthew 3:13–15,

Jesus arrived from Galilee at the Jordan, coming to John, to be baptized by him. But John tried to prevent Him, saying, *"I need to be baptized by You, and do You come to me?"*

But Jesus answering said to him, *"Permit it at this time; for in this way it is fitting for us to fulfill all righteousness."*

Then he permitted Him. Jesus was talking of those who came before HIM; it was the only way they could be forgiven.

The Apostles understood the *place value of the 2 Baptisms.*

Through them, those who believed in Jesus Christ and converted unto faith were taught how to worship and serve God. They directed them (church) in their walk of faith, thus how to abide in the *pattern,* which Jesus came to establish within and through Himself, being the *record of faith.*

Jesus Christ WAS and IS the pattern for faith, the prototype as the Firstborn, so that all whom believe(d) in Him could enter INTO Him by the baptism of the Spirit, for Him to be IN them, and thus through Jesus they were also in the Father as ONE. That is the unity of the Spirit.

The Father in the Son; the Son in the father; the Son in us and us in Him. Thus the church worships Him in *ONE faith, ONE Spirit and ONE truth.* Through the stewardship of the Apostles, they accepted and labored with the record for faith that consisted of: *the authorized, sanctified terms God determined in order for Jesus to stand as the Mediator before God for those of faith, each time they touched the contact points for the New Covenant; *the commandments and tokens; *the spiritual contact points, that sets the boundaries for faith.

Thus they were IN Christ, by touching the things sanctified by the sprinkling of His blood upon it.

This is easy to understand if explained by comparison, looking at an everyday life situation. As an example we can look at someone seeking to do a *carpenters job. Firstly*, in order for him (student/ trainee artisan) to do his work in an *acceptable, profitable and perfect manner*, he must want to be a carpenter. No joy is found in doing something you don't want to do, right?

Then he has to receive tutoring in how to be a carpenter, meaning he has to be trained. He is trained by knowledgeable qualified appointed people in an institution of learning or place of employment where he will qualify as a carpenter on acceptance of what will be expected of him when in training and the standard for his qualification that has been determined. He is taught the art of his craft. He is taught what tools to use and how to use them for his benefit and the benefit of his future employer, in order to produce creative furniture or works of art to beautify or fulfill a specific function, its by the tools and the wood that he is able to produce through his labor what is required from him by his employer.

This, taken back to faith in covenant, is exactly what has to happen with each repentant sinner, baptized in the Holy Spirit, whereby the now righteous saint, will *study the doctrine of Christ* to be *approved of God* under qualified appointed stewards, by being equipped to function in the fullness of Christ in the body of Christ Jesus.

Knowledge is needed for faith, under inspiration and through the power of God's Spirit and the spiritual Law of Grace and Truth.

This is needed for the perfecting of the soul, in beauty (virtue/ fruit) through functioning in the priesthood of Jesus Christ.

Phil 2:12 says,

"...work out your own salvation in fear and trembling"

Thus, "partake of Me, abide in Me and be approved of Me, keeping Me in remembrance as ye labor at the altar of righteousness, bearing My yoke, for each man chooses whether he lives or dies."

When we know God in truth, we fear the withdrawal of His grace - and the power of His Spirit of Truth, because when we are ONE in Him, we know Him, as we are in Him and know the power that brought Jesus Christ back to life. (fear and trembling) Faith is cognitive. Faith is by will.

Faith carries a responsibility that is the activity (do righteousness according to His standard) of faith, to be reborn in Jesus Christ as we are baptized INTO His death.

The power of salvation is not through water, but *by the Spirit only.*

The days of the church sitting on the sidelines argumenting as each seeks their own glory and honor, shrugging their responsibility towards God, is GONE.

The church stands independent from God, not IN His truth.

The church has enmity with God, they are not at peace with God and know not His peace within that enables the saints to *bear all things, endure all things, hope all things and believe all things.* (1 Cor 13:7)

No one will be able to claim innocence through ignorance of His truth on the Day of the Lord.

Truth opens the eyes and unclogs the ears, when the Spirit is the inspiration that empowers faith.

Truth offends the protesters and the disobedient. But although it might be foolish to the world, it's *the bread of life* to those who partake of Him and abide in Him, who are the *consenters* of His plan for salvation.

"But woe unto those who resist the grace of the Lord, for His judgments shall never the less befall the children of disobedience, as He glorifies and exalt the children of obedience unto their eternal reward."

The Apostles were authorized by God to teach His ordered doctrine and by the measure of grace (Eph 4:7) -

"7 But unto every one of us is given grace according to the measure of the gift of Christ "upon their calling. They kept the Body of Christ in *remembrance of their responsibility to God* as they taught them the doctrine (truth) of Christ. They were able to "rightly divide" the word of God (2 Tim 2:15),

"15 Study to shew thyself approved unto God, a workman that needeth not to be ashamed, rightly dividing the word of truth",

which means they had discernment of the spiritual things hidden to the carnal mind and could compare the 2 kingdoms at work (2 Tim 2:7),

"7 Consider what I say; and the Lord give thee understanding in all things as the Spirit of God was within them" (Eph 4:6)

"6 One God and Father of all, who is above all, and through all, and in you all." Those whom was baptized with the Holy Spirit and walked after the Rhythm of the Spirit in covenant, were given the gift of discernment by the grace and truth of God, through their labor in the priesthood 1 Pet 2:5 & 9

"5 Ye also, as lively stones, are built up a spiritual house, a holy priesthood, to offer up spiritual sacrifices, acceptable to God by Jesus Christ.

9 But ye are a chosen generation, a royal priesthood, a holy nation, a peculiar people; that ye should shew forth the praises of him who hath called you out of darkness into his marvelous light;" - of which Jesus was/is the High Priest. Spiritual things can only be spiritually discerned by the spiritually minded, who abide in Jesus Christ and have the Spirit within.

God protected His knowledge from being defiled and the value of His truth being lost by setting all things for salvation IN Jesus Christ our Lord, within a framework of truth, and making the Baptism of the Spirit a necessary step in order for those whom believe in Him, to be reborn. Titus 3:5

"5 Not by works of righteousness which we have done, but according to his mercy he saved us, by the washing of regeneration, and renewing of the Holy Ghost; in and through Jesus Christ's Death and Resurrection."

Phil 1:21

"For to me to live is Christ, and to die is gain."

When in the Spirit we die daily to the self(old man) and are born anew unto the new man, as Christ Jesus is formed within us, through bearing of fruit unto virtue, which is the power of God through Jesus Christ. This is the substance of Christ, and this is the reason why we have to be baptized in the Spirit, for without the Spirit, this divine transformation cannot take place through the Operation of God by *grace and truth* (Divine power), whereby we take on His likeness through this *process of regeneration unto renewing of the mind.*

Renewing the mind is to have the mind of Jesus Christ, which means, we see through His eyes (not literally) which means, we have His perspective. We are in the same mind, in the same perspective and in *agreement* with HIM as we co-labour with Him in building His House. When our perspective changes, we will no longer be deceived by the prince of the power of the air as we walk in the liberty of Jesus Christ (justified) freed from the power of sin unto death. Eph 2:2

"Wherein in the past ye walked according to the course of the world (flesh empowered by false knowledge), according to the prince of the power of the air (antiChrist spirit), the spirit that now worketh in the children of disobedience:" Eph 2:3

"...fulfilling the desires of the flesh and of the MIND: and were by nature the children of wrath, even as others."

By the baptism of the Spirit, we become the children of mercy, vessels of righteousness.

We can see in reading the New Testament that the Baptism of the Spirit was given as a commandment issued to the Apostles, *to go forth and baptize in the name of the Father, the Son and the Holy Ghost.*

The church is confused and misdirected in their walk of faith by the deceitful interpretation and application of scripture, that comes through the vain imaginations of men that have created their own acceptable traditions for faith's experience, the likes of those included, who seek God on their own and privately interpret the gospel, without the Holy Spirit to bear witness to Jesus, whilst remaining outside the framework given for faith. Remaining within the restrictions, increased understanding of the Hidden mystery of Jesus Christ is gained, but definitely not whilst you remain independent from God.

The point made here, is that the Apostles didn't follow their own dogma, they followed the gospel of Jesus Christ in Covenant, by the spiritual Law of Grace and Truth, laboring with the authorized things within a certain environment (the womb of His covenant) that was determined by God for perfect faith.

This applies to the church today as well, 2000+ years later. God hasn't added anything new for this time period and He hasn't taken anything away either, for He is, was and always will be true to His Word.

The Apostles didn't tell converters they could choose what to do, what to touch and what to believe in. For them to be IN Christ, they had to conform to His knowledge as truth penetrated their hearts AND be one with the Father and the Son through the baptism of the Spirit, which then unite the body of Christ in one mind, one truth, one faith and in one Spirit in order for them to receive the blessings of Jesus Christ, that is spiritual and not carnal. The Apostles taught wholesome doctrine as received by Jesus Christ, whom gave them the commandment to go forth into the world and baptize *"in the Name of the Father, the Son and the Holy Ghost,* as they followed the direction of God through Christ for faith in Him and were baptized in the Spirit (seal) that was the entrance into covenant faith.

Mt.28:19 as a command from Jesus.

"Go therefore, and teach all nations, baptizing them in the NAME of the FATHER, SON, and HOLY GHOST."

The Apostles never confirmed water baptism to be a prerequisite for salvation, but for confession of faith and repentance of sins yes!

Should the Church baptize in water using the name of Jesus, or should they use the name of the Father, Son and the Holy Ghost?

In the times of the Apostles, no contradiction existed to the value of the baptism of the Spirit, for they were given the measure of grace, by which they taught the doctrine, kept it pure and direct the faith of the church on the tracks of truth.

In the absence of teaching apostles, the church does not know what the NAME of JESUS means, as well-meaning, zealous men/women, without that measure of grace, are dictating policy for the church without understanding and authority. The tares have led the wheat on a wrong path through their man made religious philosophies and so the church endures a walk of faith that lacks the power of divine change by the divine power of God, not knowing the Lord in righteousness.

Acts 2:38,

"Repent, and be baptized (water) every one of you in the name of Jesus Christ FOR (looking forward to) the remission of sins (that would come through the baptism of the Holy Spirit)."

Whenever scripture speaks of 'THE NAME OF' it's NOT the "speaking of the name" or names given, but what they embody.

THE NAME: Represents the framework of the one who embodies your salvation. What the Father, Son, and Holy Spirit embody collectively, they all embody individually.

The FATHER ---- Where the plan of salvation originated.

The SON - -------- Came out from the Father to become the plan of God

The Holy Spirit --- Fulfills the plan of God in the hearts of those who believe.

Thus, One God manifesting Himself in 3 ways: The Father, Son, and Holy Spirit all embody the same plan and work within the same framework of truth, and through one baptism that God uses as the point of access to the soul.

Those who were baptized in water in the name of Jesus were making a public confession of the plan that Jesus embodied through His death and resurrection. They are giving testimony that they are in agreement with the plan of salvation that the Father, Son, and the Holy Spirit embody as ONE. They were undergoing a symbolic expression through the baptism of water that pointed to the baptism to come. The Baptism of the Spirit.

The one submitting to water baptism also confesses to be a disciple of Jesus, and therefore professes that he will join with God in covenant through receiving the baptism that Jesus Himself gives---- the baptism of the Holy Spirit.

God embodies not only the plan, but the work of redemption. God intended to officiate over the work of redemption personally in the soul of man. This is the purpose of the baptism of the Holy Spirit. This baptism allows the point of access to the soul. Now God embodies the work of His plan through the power of His Spirit WITHIN the believer. The Father, Son, and Holy Spirit are in great expectation of ONE work to be done within through the purging, healing and cleansing of regeneration (Titus 3:5; 1 Thes 2:13/ 2 Pet 1.3), that takes place within the soul by the effectual working power of the Holy Spirit as truth penetrates the heart.

When we say and do things that is not within the framework of His truth, then we are not to be found IN Him, and therefore we are not OF Him, for what we then do does not confirm Jesus Christ, as the evidence we give in the name of Jesus is confirming another gospel, another Jesus (a simulated version of the Original, in name only) and another spirit (unholy spirit). The application of water has NO effect on sin.

The Baptism of water was a mere forerunner of what was to come, the Baptism of the Holy Spirit by fire. It's through this baptism that remission of sins were/are received, through the Operation of God within.

God never intended the baptism of water to replace the baptism of the Spirit. Regeneration is initiated for the birth of Jesus Christ WITHIN (new man).

Water had its place, it was to be only a temporary measure for a certain period in time, to be done by John on repentance of sin and confession of faith by disciples of John's preaching of Jesus to come, it symbolically pointed to the baptism of the Spirit and the power thereof.

The hearts of believers were prepared by the preaching of John the Baptist, who was the witness for Jesus Christ to come.

In Luke 3:16 (KJV), John the Baptist says:

"John answered, saying unto them all, I indeed baptize you with water; but one mightier than I cometh, the latchet of whose shoes I am not worthy to unloose: he shall baptize you with the Holy Ghost and with fire:"

First: here John clearly states, he baptizes with water (a physical act). This took place after confession of faith by those who believed. They believed the preaching of John, whom preached salvation through Christ Jesus. Remission of sins did NOT take place through that baptism, but it gave believers the opportunity to confess their faith, in expectation of being baptized in the Spirit.

If the water baptism were perfect, there would be no need for the Baptism of the Spirit, would there?

It's only by and through the Spirit of the Law of Grace and Truth, that the new man is born.

We die IN Christ, and we are resurrected IN Him and THROUGH Him to be OF Him.

Secondly he bears witness of Jesus Christ being the One that will baptize in the Spirit.

He says, "one MIGHTER than I cometh" who is Jesus Christ. It follows this pattern, first the water, then the Spirit.

Let's look at the following scriptures:

Acts 11:16 (KJV)

"Then remembered I the word of the Lord, how that he said, John indeed baptized with water; but ye shall be baptized with the Holy Ghost"

Can believers dispute the words of the Lord?

If so, are they choosing what to believe and what not to believe?

What to accept and what to reject?

Is the Word of God in part?? Is salvation in part??

When believers walk each after their own vain imaginations, then that which Jesus came to set in Himself as a whole, is seen in part, expressed in part, and understood in part. Plainly said, something is missing. They can't SEE. They can't HEAR.

The Spirit makes faith living, as it bears witness to the record of faith, who IS Jesus Christ. The power in Jesus is within the things we handle, touch and taste of when we partake of Him in His priesthood. Our faith is empowered by the things we labor with, the Spirit we submit too through due diligence(labor with contact points), consistency(labor with truth) and communication(prayer) that strengthens our faith in righteousness, as we are humbled by grace through which we see the face of Jesus, in all things.

We can liken it to the following:

A man has a car(faith) in his garage that he doesn't often uses(no responsibility), but every Sunday(law of Moses; the flesh, tradition of men) he goes into his garage(church), dusts and polishes the car, open the bonnet and inspect the car inside and out, then he gets behind the steering-wheel of the car, switches on the ignition(inspiration of the spirit of the world) and let the car idle, touching all the things that he would have had to use to operate the car(activity of faith and works of the flesh), IF he was actually driving, whilst he is imagining(tradition of men) he is driving down a lane of beautiful green trees towards the coast(experience of faith) he can feel the wind in his hair, he feels the excitement of the trip(experience of faith), but his car(faith) is going nowhere(faith in vain), because the car is idling(absence of eyes of body of Christ) on an empty fuel tank(, the fumes of petrol lingering in the tank, giving it a spark of life. (Holy Ghost without, not within)

1 Corinthians 12:13 (KJV)

"For by one Spirit are we all baptized into one body, whether we be Jews or Gentiles, whether we be bond or free; and have been all made to drink into one Spirit."

"One Spirit" – no mention of water, it's not saying; "For by one water", no it says, One Spirit. Confirming the Holy Spirit to be the baptism by which the Body has to be baptized with.

"into one body"– herewith understood, that by the One Spirit of Life, the body is brought into unity. Unity of the Spirit, wherein the Father is in the Son, as He is in the Father and as we are in the Son, so we are in the Father.

United as ONE - BY the Spirit of truth.

The body stands in agreement with God in all things that He has sanctified for faith and sprinkled with the blood of Christ.

Unity – complete agreement, something whole that is made of parts

Wow! Isn't this amazing? This is exactly what happens when we are baptized with the Holy Spirit, into the Body of Christ.

We are joined together, to become one thing, one body. The perfect bride of Christ, without spot or wrinkle; a virtuous woman whose price is far above that of rubies. She glorifies her Husband and mates for the increase of His House.

The Bride stands in total agreement with her Husband, for so they have become ONE.

When the body stands in agreement with Jesus, as said before, they are in one mind and in one accord, this is the equity of the Lord restored to the innerman and to the body as a whole. The body has many members (parts) but all function together for the benefit of the Head, through which He leads the body in His ways.

"made too" – enforcement of a commandment – this is the way, no other way. Only ONE has the authority to set commandments.

This is His good pleasure that those who believe shall drink of the Spirit and be filled with Him. To never be thirsty again.

"into One Spirit" – into = moving inside of something or some place We enter INTO Jesus by the baptism of the Spirit, we are IN Him, and we are hidden IN Him. This is what it means to abide in Him. Once we drink, we are united IN the Spirit by the Spirit. We are now partaking of His substance to take on the likeness of Christ, as God brings healing to the soul through circumcision of the heart by the working of the Spirit of grace and truth.

In Romans 6:3

"3. Know ye not, that so many of us were baptized INTO Jesus Christ were baptized INTO His death?

4 Therefore we are buried with him by baptism into death: that like Christ was raised up from the dead by the glory of the Father, even so we also should walk in the newness of life.

5 For if we have been planted together in the likeness of his death, we shall be also in the likeness of his resurrection:"

"INTO Jesus Christ " - As we are baptized with the Spirit, we enter INTO Jesus Christ. This speaks of the unity of the Spirit, for unity of the body, laboring with His knowledge and tokens for faith. We are within Him, He is within us. We cannot be united with God through Jesus Christ without the Baptism taking place. Spiritual things are only compared to spiritual things and this is only possible for those who have drunk from the well of the Spirit.

"Into His death" - We die with Him on receiving the seal (baptism). This means that we will be following the pattern for faith that Jesus came to establish for the church to follow.

His death and resurrection is the power of our salvation. Dying to the self (flesh) to be resurrected unto the new life (spiritual man). The end of the old man begins when we are baptized.

As we are then resurrected by the same power that brought Him back to life on the 3rd day, it is the beginning (birth) of the new man, being reborn through the Spirit that quickens.

We are then freed from the bondage of the flesh, to enter into the liberty of Jesus Christ, we are now free to act in God's best interest (justified), and that is to build His House and increase His kingdom eternally through fruit bearing unto virtue. "Freed from the bondage of the flesh" means that we are being separated by the seal from our labor with the knowledge and wisdom of this world that works iniquity and is by the law of sin unto death, to labor now with the knowledge of His truth, using the tokens of our activity of faith, sanctified by His blood.

There is no condemnation in Jesus Christ, for condemnation came by the Law of Moses (10 commandments), but in covenant the Lord writes His commandments on the tables of our hearts and as we take on His likeness, we do no sin. Our transgressions are forgiven through our activity of faith daily, meaning our consistency of labor with His knowledge as we touch Him for purging, healing and cleansing by our labor with the spiritual contact points and tokens for faith. But the Lord *does* set righteous judgments for correction and chastisement when needed.

We do not receive a new soul on conversion, we enter into Him with the fruits of iniquity still present and through regeneration, the soul is healed from the scars caused by sin through our new habit of faith.

Through this process, remembrance of sin and the pain and suffering endured are removed through the Law of grace and truth, as we submit to His Spirit and are humbled by grace unto circumcision of the heart.

So you see, regeneration is an everyday process taking place, not a once off procedure. This process is ignited through our labor of serving Him in word and indeed.

Being transformed into a new creature in Christ, we bear the mark of Christ in the soul.

His mark is virtue.

Virtue is the only acceptable currency, if you wish, that is accepted by God. For by this mark of Christ within, we are known to be of Him.

A transition has to take place, from flesh to Flame (Spirit).

Very important to remember, is that Divine transformation (due process of regeneration) comes only through Divine power, no physical water washing or dunking has the power to bring forth this transformation.

To recap: Water washing (cleansing) points symbolically, to the work of regeneration (Operation of God).

As said before, water baptism is a physical deed that points to the baptism of the Spirit and the power thereof to bring forth new life within the soul.

Cleansing and transformation comes by the power of God, His Spirit that is the Spirit of Life.

In John 3: 3, we read,

"That which is born of the flesh is the flesh; and that which is born of the Spirit is spirit."

Contrast of darkness and light, death and life, being without His power and being within His power through the Spirit, thus saying, the Spirit is without (flesh) - and the Spirit is within the body."

1 Cor 6:19

"What? Know ye not that your body is the temple of the Holy Ghost which is in you, which ye have of God, and ye are not your own?"

The pattern (Death + Resurrection): to die to the old (flesh) and to be born again (re-enter) into the womb of His covenant wherein we remain united and enjoined with God through Jesus Christ.

Therefore, to recap, this refers to the dying of the old man (natural man/ the flesh) to be resurrected IN Him through the same power by which He was resurrected, the power of the Spirit of God, unto the new man (spiritual man). Thus, this speaks of being REBORN by the death AND the resurrection of Christ. THIS is the power of our salvation that is IN and THROUGH Jesus Christ, for taking on the very substance of Jesus Christ (His virtue), the Lord our God is well pleased, for he sees the reflection of His Son within us. Without this reflection, we will not be accepted by Him to be of Him.

"Newness of Life" – once again, it is by the spiritual Law of grace and truth, that we are separated from the world unto the Lord within His covenant, doing righteousness (serving Him in word and indeed), while we remain within the framework of truth.

Within the framework we are restricted to the terms for our contact with Him and expression of faith.

2 Cor 5:17

"Therefore if any man be in Christ, he is a new creature: old things are passed away; behold, all things are become new"

Acts 11:16 (KJV)

"Then remembered the word of the Lord, how that he said, John indeed baptized with water; but ye shall be baptized with the Holy Ghost."

"that he said" – referring to Jesus. Jesus said, "but ye shall be baptized with the Holy Ghost". This is His standard, "ye shall be"…the word of Jesus speaks truth and in His word we abide.

John 1:1

"In the beginning was the Word, (originated) - The Father and the Word was with God (Initiated)-The Son and the Word was God"(sustained) – The Holy Ghost

The Word of God became flesh = Jesus Christ, in whom the power of God is set.

Reading Math 11:27 Jesus said;

"All things are delivered unto me of my Father: and no man knoweth the Son, but the Father; neither knoweth any man the Father, save the Son, and he to whomsoever the Son will reveal him"

"All things are delivered unto me of my Father" – Jesus says He is the will of the Father and in Him is the authority of God. Those given to Him by His Father so they can be saved by His blood, will know Him and be of Him, but also He says, no man knows Him. It is applicable to those who are not in unity of the Spirit, thus they who are not sealed with the baptism of the Spirit.

To recap: We can only know Him when we are in the Spirit. At the time of His ministry, the Spirit was not within believers by the baptism, only after He was transcended did they receive the Spirit of life and fire. No man will know Jesus through carnal understanding and the baptism of water, because spirituality can only be compared and understood through and by the spiritual and the spiritual minded, which are they who are baptized with the Spirit of The Lord. When so baptized, we will know God through Jesus Christ, as they are One, because we are then in Jesus as we drink deeply into the Spirit and thus we will thirst no more.

To know God and His will, is to walk in righteousness that is imputed upon those who enter His covenant and are born of the Spirit.

"and he to whomsoever the Son will reveal him" –"Many are called but few are chosen."

God reveals Jesus to those who are willing to be humbled to His grace and yield to the Spirit. This means God reveals Jesus Christ to the seeking heart, in Truth, after which repentance is sealed by the Baptism of the Spirit. When Jesus Christ is revealed by grace, and we respond in faith, we are found righteous before God, and then we are sealed with the baptism.

Not all men will accept the revelation of Jesus Christ by the power of Grace, because truth does offend the proud and high-minded. Therefore Jesus said, *to whomsoever He will*, because if your heart is not humbled to grace, you will never know Him, even if you are called.

God knowing the beginning from the end knows who shall accept or reject Him. Therefore, *"many is called, but few are chosen"*(2 Pet 3:18)

Acts 18:27 – *"helped them much which had believed through grace"*

2 Cor 6: 1 - *"We then, as workers together with Him, beseech you that ye receive not the grace of God in vain."*

Eph 2:5 - *"Even we were dead in sins, hath quickened us together with Christ, (by grace ye are saved)"*

Jas 4:6 - *"but he giveth more grace, wherefore he saith, God resisteth the proud, but giveth grace unto the humble."*

1 Pet 5:5 – *"for God resisteth the proud and giveth grace unto the humble"*

1 Pet 5:12 – *"testifying, that this is the true grace of God wherein ye stand"*

True grace is the power of God (Voice) that calls the world out of darkness unto Himself and that nurtures and sustains the soul after the seal, to grow in grace daily through co-labourer with Christ. The grace of God is His Voice calling forth those whom He choose to reveal Himself too albeit all is called, for only the humble will yield to grace and submit to the effectual working power if the Spirit, that makes faith and living experience, wherein the fullness of Christ is the reality if faith.

The voice of God spoke and said, *"This is My Son in whom I am well pleased"* as the Spirit in the form of a dove descended upon Jesus, after the water baptism. This was God's voice (grace) that revealed Jesus as the Son of God, for He walked in the will of His father. So too does God reveal Jesus to the humble, who stand in that revelation and believe, thus in humbleness the heart responds in faith, to be found righteous before the Lord.

Grace is not the UNMERITED favor of God. He reveals His Son only and by the Spirit bears witness of Him, so we can believe in him.

As He and the Father are ONE, so He fulfilled the will of God within and through Himself. Jesus said many times, *"these things I Speak are not of Myself, but from My Father"*. He is and was the authority of God on earth. He did the will of His Father, seeking not to affirm Himself in power, but kept in mind the plan of God for salvation that came through Jesus Christ. He fulfilled everything of the Law of Moses within Himself. That which was old was replaced by the new, that of death by that which is of life. The law pointed to Jesus Christ in part, but He fulfilled it in Himself as a whole.

The covenant of the flesh (Moses), replaced by the covenant of the Spirit (Jesus); Transitioning the church from dead works of faith (works of contrition) to works of faith (Spirit).

Luke 12:50(KJV)

50 But I have a baptism to be baptized with; and how am I straightened till it is accomplished!"

"The baptism of John, was it from heaven, or of men?

The baptism of water by John the Baptist was for repentance of sins only after confession of faith, until He came to baptize with the Spirit. It's His Spirit that enters into the body, to sojourn there.

The symbolism carries no power, but the reality of the Spirit does.

God authorized this water ritual in preparation for the baptism of Life, so those who believed the preaching of John, could confess faith and repent, symbolically showing outwardly the washing, healing and cleansing of the soul, by the Spirit of Truth. That what was to come, was the reality, not the water ritual.

John did not act by his own council, but acted on the word of God that came to Him.

The tradition of the Jews was to wash for cleansing before certain feasts and rituals; this was done at the same time John started to preach at the river Jordan.

It brings to mind the following:

Water as an element on the periodic table and the workhorse of the earth, has been used by God for certain purposes to exact certain results throughout the history as written of in the Bible.

The first important incident of water being used in a mighty way, was when God cleansed the earth by water through the flood (1st consummation) (Gen 6-7), removing all that was evil and defiled from the earth(Gen 6: 5-7, 13,17/ Gen 7:23), but those He chose to be saved as Noah (Noah & his family because of Noah's righteousness: Gen 6:18) found grace in God's eyes(Gen 6: 8), were saved in the ark(Gen 6:14;18 / Gen 7:16) to be the prototype of life(Gen 8:15-18) that would come from them, carrying them away on the waters for 40 days and 40 nights(time of purging and cleansing), as it rained.

The second great work that involved water was through the opening of the Red Sea as the Israelites were led out of Egypt. The waters were divided with a wall on both sides for the Israelites to pass through on dry land, under stewardship of Moses, as he was chosen by God and found to be righteous, because of his obedience through faith. This symbolized their baptism, being carried forth from bondage (Egypt) unto liberty (Canaan), but they too had to go through a time of purging and cleansing before they could enter the Promised Land. (Exodus 14: 21-22)

The third one involving water is in Exodus 17: 5-6 the water from the rock. God told Moses to take the same rod with which he smote the river and smote the rock in His presence, when Moses did that, there came forth water from the rock that quenched the thirst of His people and all with them.

Jesus Christ is the Rock from which proceeds the living water that quenches the thirst of those who partake of Him. By the living waters of the Spirit, we are brought in the presence of the Father and the Son within us and us in them; Partaking of the fullness of Jesus Christ. This is the reality of faith in Him; this is the reality of the power of His Spirit of life.

The fourth important one involving water is in John 2:1-10, *And the third day there was a marriage in Cana of Galilee; and the mother of Jesus was there:*

2 And both Jesus was called, and his disciples, to the marriage. 3 And when they wanted wine, the mother of Jesus saith unto him, They have no wine.

4 Jesus saith unto her, Woman, what have I to do with thee? Mine hour has not yet come.

5 His mother saith unto the servants, whatsoever he saith unto you, do it.

6 And there were set there six water-pots of stone, after the manner of the purifying of the Jews, containing two or three firkins apiece. 7 Jesus saith unto them, Fill the water-pots with water. And they filled them up to the brim.

8 And he saith unto them, Draw out now, and bear unto the governor of the feast. And they bare it.

9 When the ruler of the feast had tasted the water that was made of wine, and knew not whence it was: (but the <u>servants</u> who drew the water knew;) the governor of the feast called the bridegroom,

10 And saith unto him, Every man at the beginning doth set forth good wine; and when men have well drunk, then that which is worse: but <u>thou hast kept the good wine</u> until now."

This was the first miracle that Jesus Christ performed. Changing of water that was to be used for ritual cleansing at the wedding, into the sweetest wine, better than what was ever tasted by those attending the wedding function.

This symbolically speaks of the wine (knowledge) of the vine (Jesus Christ) by which we are sustained (strengthened in faith), as the branches (believers) are engrafted (baptism of the Spirit) into the vine (Jesus), what proceeded forth was the substance of Christ (virtue) within the fruit the branches beareth. The branches were nurtured by what proceeded from the vine, and thus were adopted (baptism of the Spirit) to be of the true vine.

Let's look first at verse 6

JOHN established the setting for Jesus to act. He tells the audience about the presence of six water jars there in the scene (John 2:6). The phrase "for the purification rituals of the Jews" explains why the jars are there. He focuses our attention on the jars long enough to point out considerable detail, six, count them 6 jars made of stone not clay. The most important part of this is they were the kind the JEWS used for ceremonial washing. These jars were all about religious activity. This was the law in those times cleansing by water. So when JESUS turned this water into wine what is the real secret of what HE was showing us? See the water that was to cleanse but JESUS was turning it into HIS blood to show us it was only through HIM after HIS death on the cross, that the water that was for cleansing, was now HIS blood.

Why else would HE say this in verse 4,

"Jesus saith unto her, Woman, what have I to do with thee? mine hour has not yet come."

See, this was at the start of HIS ministry HE knew HE would have to show signs and wonders for them to believe. Let's look at this.

JOHN 4

46 So Jesus came again into Cana of Galilee, where he made the water wine. And there was a certain nobleman, whose son was sick at Capernaum.

47 When he heard that Jesus was coming out of Judea into Galilee, he went unto him, and besought him that he would come down, and heal his son: for he was at the point of death.

48 Then said Jesus unto him, Except ye see signs and wonders, ye will not believe. See this man was probably at that wedding and saw what JESUS did when HIS son was dying he came to JESUS.

The six pots represent the days GOD created the world the water which under the law was for sin all now are now t JESUS only. John 14 6Jesus said to him, "I am the way, and the truth, and the life; no one comes to the Father but through Me.

Mark 7:1-4King James Version (KJV)

7 Then came together unto him the Pharisees, and certain of the scribes, which came from Jerusalem.

2 And when they saw some of his disciples eat bread defiled, that is to say, with unwashed hands, they found fault.

3 for the Pharisees, and all the Jews, except they wash their hands oft, eat not, holding the tradition of the elders.

4 And when they come from the market, except they wash, they eat not. And many other things there are, which they have received to hold, such as the washing of cups, pots, brazen vessels, and of tables."

But, through JESUS showing us what was going to happen on the cross here HE CLEARLY shows it's only through HIM we can be saved.

The water of cleansing, physical pure water symbolizes the baptism of John that enabled those that believed in Him, to symbolically say: we repented of our sins and will yield to the cleaning, purging and healing of the baptism that is to come, in which we are in expectation of. They were symbolically separated by this ritual, but had not the reality of Jesus Christ yet, as remission of sins could not yet take place, until the true baptism that has the power of transformation from the old to the new; from death unto life; from ignorance to understanding.

Clearly, the water of nature has been used in powerful ways and in symbolic ways, but none hold the power to bring forth the new man in Christ Jesus, only the Spirit of God can bring forth life from out of death, thus the dead are resurrected by the power of God unto life.

In John 3, 1- 8 we read, about Nicodemus

"1. There was a man of the Pharisees named Nicodemus, a ruler of the Jews.

2 This man came to Jesus at night and said to Him, "Rabbi, we know that You are a teacher come from God; for no one can do these signs that You do unless God is with him."

3. Jesus answered and said to him, "Most assuredly, I say to you, unless one is born again, he cannot see the kingdom of God." 4. Nicodemus said to Him, "How can a man be born when he is old? Can he enter a second time into his mother's womb and be born?"

5. Jesus answered, "Most assuredly, I say to you, unless one is born of water and the Spirit, he cannot enter the kingdom of God.

6. That which is born of the flesh is flesh, and that which is born of the Spirit is spirit. 7. Do not marvel that I said to you, "You must be born again.'

8. The wind blows where it wishes, and you hear the sound of it, but cannot tell where it comes from and where it goes. So is everyone who is born of the Spirit."

People taking the stance that water baptism is necessary for salvation will say, "See, and look here! This verse says that 'unless one is born of water and the Spirit, he cannot enter into the kingdom of God.'"

What does "born of water" mean?

Is this phrase referring to water baptism?

In verse 1, Nicodemus is asking Jesus how he can possibly enter back into his mother's womb and be re-born.

So he's thinking about physical birth.

Being carnal minded, he wasn't in the position to understand the concept of being physically re-born and thus had no idea what Jesus was actually talking about. He could not discern, as he had not the Spirit within him.

Jesus wasn't talking about physical rebirth; He was referring to spiritual rebirth through the baptism of the Spirit. Entering into the womb of His covenant by which the old man was reborn as the new man.

Verses 5 & 6:

"Most assuredly, I say to you, unless one is born of water and the Spirit, he cannot enter the kingdom of God.

That which is born of the flesh is flesh, and that which is born of the Spirit is spirit." "unless one is born of water and the Spirit"

We are born into the dimension of waters, physically protected in a womb filled with nurturing waters for the duration of our stay therein, until being born in due time.

Therefore we are born into the kingdom of the flesh, as vessels of flesh. Our only way back to God who created us, is through the process of transformation (regeneration of the soul), by the baptism of the Spirit.

Unless physically born and then spiritually reborn, entering into Christ and thus also the Father, we won't be accepted by God for our return home.

If you're physically born, you're just a lost human born into sin and death.

If you're spiritually reborn, you've entered into a relationship with Jesus Christ, co-laboring with Him, being prisoners of Him, as we carry the yoke of His knowledge, taking on His likeness through regeneration AND THE BIRTH of Him within, which is His virtue formed within the soul. *Divine transformation by Divine power for forming of spiritual fruit (virtue) = Regeneration*

Reading from Titus 5:3,

"Not by works of righteousness which we have done, but according to his mercy he saved us, by the washing of regeneration, and renewing of the Holy Ghost.

A very important word in this scripture is regeneration, "by the washing of Regeneration." Regeneration means being born again. How are we born again?

Only, through JESUS CHRIST.

Regeneration is part of the "SALVATION PACKAGE".

Another word for Regeneration is Rebirth, from which we get the phrase "born again". To be born again is opposite to, and distinguished from, our first birth, when we were conceived into sin. The new birth is a SPIRITUAL, HOLY, and Divine birth, signified by being made alive in a spiritual sense. Our first birth, on the other hand, was one of spiritual death because of inherited sin. Man in his natural state is "dead in trespass and sin" until we are made alive - "Regenerated" by CHRIST when we place our faith in HIM and express it in word and deed.

Ephesians 2 King James Version (KJV)

"2 And you hath he quickened, who were dead in trespasses and sins;

2 Wherein in time past ye walked according to the course of this world, according to the prince of the power of the air, the spirit that now worketh in the children of disobedience:

3 Among whom also we all had our conversation in times past in the lusts of our flesh, fulfilling the desires of the flesh and of the mind; and were by nature the children of wrath, even as others."

The bible is clear that the only means of regeneration is by faith in the finished works of JESUS CHRIST, on the cross. No amount of good works or keeping of the law can regenerate the heart which from birth is "deceitful and wicked above all things"

Jeremiah 17:9 (KJV)

"The heart is deceitful above all things, and desperately wicked: who can know it" Regeneration of the soul is needed for Salvation. Paul explains this concept perfectly in Galatians 2 20, *"I am crucified with Christ: nevertheless I live; yet not I, but Christ liveth in me: and the life which I now live in the flesh I live by the faith of the Son of God, who loved me, and gave himself for me."*

This is true Regeneration. See, no man or woman, can by any carnal works - including Baptizing of water, doing of good deeds and works towards others – be saved, for it is only by the Baptism into the death of JESUS CHRIST that you can receive salvation. it is the water that flowed from HIS side on the cross that cleanses you and the blood that paid for your sins

"Washing of regeneration" – Regeneration is the likeness of Christ being formed within us, through our activity of faith, as God heals the soul from the scars of iniquity afflicted upon the soul through our contact with the false knowledge system that Satan has designed for our functioning in this world. This separates us from God. But God brings healing to the soul through circumcising the soul, which is by the power of the Spirit.

Through regeneration the new life of Christ is expressed through us, as Christ is formed within us.

Regeneration is the due process of fruit bearing unto virtue that reflects the Son perfectly, who is in the Father, for so we are in the Son, as He is within His Father.

Without this process, we won't be reborn and the soul will be absent of virtue and thus, will not be accepted by God, for His standard is Jesus Christ, seeing His reflection of virtue in us, we will be known of Him.

Let's look at yet another common verse used to defend the idea that the salvation of our souls requires (only) water baptism.

*Acts 2:38

Then Peter said to them,

"Repent, and let every one of you be baptized in the name of Jesus Christ for the remission of sins; and you shall receive the gift of the Holy Spirit."

*The Great Commission is in Matthew 28:19 - 20 records Jesus's words to His disciples, to *"go and make disciples of all the nations, baptizing them in the name of the Father and of the Son and of the Holy Spirit . . ."*

When John baptized with water, he baptized in the name of Jesus, on confession of faith and repentance. This referred to the baptism as a symbolic rite, to be fulfilled by He who would come, who would baptize with the Spirit.

But here, Jesus said, *"baptizing them in the name of the Father and of the Son and of the Holy Spirit . . ."*

This means, the baptism by which the Father, the Son and the Holy Ghost will be *in* you as you are within them. This does not refer to water baptism.

It speaks of the unity of the Spirit, that is only a reality when we are the temple of the Holy Ghost, new creatures in and through Jesus Christ our Lord.

The same can be said about Acts 2:38, the repentant believer could go through the ritual of being baptized with water, but for him to enter into Christ and experience the power of salvation unto the birth of the new man in Christ, he had to be baptized in the Spirit. Water was only a symbol and temporary measure of expressing confession and repentance before the true baptism were received. JESUS showed us their are two types of water

"7 There cometh a woman of Samaria to draw water: Jesus saith unto her, Give me to drink.

8 (For his disciples were gone away unto the city to buy meat.) 9 Then saith the woman of Samaria unto him, How is it that thou, being a Jew, askest drink of me, which am a woman of Samaria? for the Jews have no dealings with the Samaritans.

10 Jesus answered and said unto her, If thou knewest the gift of God, and who it is that saith to thee, Give me to drink; thou wouldest have asked of him, and he would have given thee living water.

11 The woman saith unto him, Sir, thou hast nothing to draw with, and the well is deep: from whence then hast thou that living water? 12 Art thou greater than our father Jacob, which gave us the well, and drank thereof himself, and his children, and his cattle? 13 Jesus answered and said unto her, whosoever drinketh of this water(physical) shall thirst again:

14 But whosoever drinketh of the water that I shall give him shall never thirst; but the water that I shall give him shall be in him a well of water springing up into everlasting life."

Which water do you want the one JESUS gives, or men??

Do not be misled, for it's clear as day and right before your eyes. Drink from the well of life and liveth eternal, returning to whence we came from. Direct your eyes heavenward and repent ye from thy transgressions against the Lord because of ignorance and be reborn into new life through Jesus Christ our Lord. For traditions of men, is the false gospel but ye that seek the lord, seek Him in truth and be saved.

Acts 8:26-40(KJV): Philip and the Eunuch

"26 And the angel of the Lord spoke unto Philip, saying, Arise, and go toward the south unto the way that goeth down from Jerusalem unto Gaza, which is desert.

27 And he arose and went: and, behold, a man of Ethiopia, an eunuch of great authority under Candace queen of the Ethiopians, who had the charge of all her treasure, and had come to Jerusalem for to worship,

28 Was returning, and sitting in his chariot reading Esaias the prophet.

29 Then the Spirit said unto Philip, Go near, and join thyself to this chariot.

30 And Philip ran thither to him, and heard him read the prophet Esaias, and said, Understandest thou what thou readest?

31 And he said, How can I, except some man, guide me? And he desired Philip to come up and sit with him. 32 The place of the scripture which he read was this, He was led as a sheep to the slaughter; and like a lamb dumb before his shearer, so opened he not his mouth:

33 In his humiliation his judgment was taken away: and who shall declare his generation? for his life is taken from the earth. 34 And the eunuch answered Philip, and said, I pray thee, of whom speaketh the prophet this? of himself, or of some other man? 35 Then Philip opened his mouth, and began at the same scripture, and preached unto him Jesus.

36 And as they went on their way, they came unto a certain water: and the eunuch said, See, here is water; what doth hinder me to be baptized?

37 And Philip said, If thou believest with all thine heart, thou mayest. And he answered and said, I believe that Jesus Christ is the Son of God.

38 And he commanded the chariot to stand still: and they went down both into the water, both Philip and the eunuch; and he baptized him.

39 And when they came up out of the water, the Spirit of the Lord caught Philip away, that the eunuch saw him no more: and he went on his way rejoicing.

40 But Philip was found at Azotus: and passing through he preached in all the cities, till he came to Caesarea"

Significantly speaking to the preachers and religious zealous ministers who preach water baptism AS the seal by which souls can experience the reality of Christ, as holy, righteous servants of the Lord. This is a false teaching covering the church in a cloak of death and futility. Where faith is in vain.

Let those who preach salvation apart from the Lord's faith through the tradition of Jesus Christ, know that they are preaching death not life.

What came to mind in reading this scripture, is that the Eunuch was in fact doing all the right things, he studied the gospel, but read it without understanding. He needed Philip as an Apostle and servant of the Lord, to preach him the truth of what was hidden in the words he read. When he heard the real meaning of what he most probably must have read many times before, he saw the "face of Christ '' in what he heard, he recognized the truth of what he heard, and he accepted (believed) what he heard as the truth too, without doubt. This revelation that came of who Jesus was, came because God's grace was present, calling him unto God…"by grace ye are saved"…grace for salvation….he then asked Philip to be baptized with water…but he could have asked for the baptism of the Spirit...but he chose water. The physical expression of being baptized without power.

It's significant that Philip was carried AWAY by the Spirit, that brought to mind the carrying away of God's righteous in the rapture, and Noah in the ark, being carried away on the waters that purged and cleansed the earth from defilement and evil in the first consummation.

What's clear to see, albeit Philip disappeared before the Eunuchs eyes, he was off rejoicing, in his mind equaling himself to Philip. But there was a difference, the one had the Spirit within and walked in faith knowing God through Jesus, the other without the Spirit.

It brings to mind the church today, believers in total ignorance professing faith and joyfully expressing their faith, but unaware of the implication of their choices made, to not be baptized in the Spirit and follow Him in truth.

What amazing about this part of the scripture is that no one seems to realize that the one who was baptized in water was <u>left behind</u>" the eunuch the one that was baptized in the water, Phillip who was not baptized in the water was <u>taken away in the Spirit,</u> something to think about.

It's time for the church to wake from their slumber!! Amen

1 Peter 2:15

"For so is the will of God, that with well doing ye may put to silence the ignorance of foolish men:"

Jesus Christ, Servant of God

The Lord's Chosen Servant

Isaiah 42:1 King James Version

"1 Behold my servant, whom I uphold; mine elect, in whom my soul delighteth; I have put my spirit upon him: he shall bring forth judgment to the Gentiles."

Isaiah 49:6 King James Version

"6 And he said, It is a light thing that thou shouldest be my servant to raise up the tribes of Jacob, and to restore the preserved of Israel: I will also give thee for a light to the Gentiles, that thou mayest be my salvation unto the end of the earth."

Jesus Christ, the Holy One, the Son of God and the Son of man, was send to this world born of flesh, to be *His Saviour* for those that He created in His image, that was born into sin and death, because of the 1st Adam that fell due to him listening, reasoning and accepting the *council of Satan* (the prince of the air) who is the *father of iniquity* and the *first father* to all born into sin.

Jesus Christ came unto His own; to save them from *sin that brought the curse of death* to their souls, for the reflection of the soul of man mirrors not the perfection of Jesus Christ, but the *corruption of Satan* through his designed system of iniquity.

God sent Himself to be the *perfect uncorrupted, spotless sacrifice*; He spilled His blood on the *cross*, to establish a covenant with His own people, whereby they can *know* Him and *fellowship* with Him being *reconciled with* - and *joined* to Him, as the *enmity* is removed, that exists between God and man due to *the breach of corruption* (death & sin), in order for them to *return* to Him in all *pureness* and *perfection*, through obedience in faith. Jesus Christ IS the bridge that crosses the breach that exists between God and man.

Jesus Christ walked in *the perfect will of His Father* and although He was a man of flesh, He was God in the flesh. He suffered under the contradictions of sinners, being called names, was persecuted by the tares and endured the frailty of a fleshly body. He was subject to heat and cold, hunger and thirst, tiredness and fatigue, but not *once* did He seek to *satisfy His own needs* or *alter circumstances*, by using His Divine powers for resolve. At all times He kept His Father in remembrance (the plan of God), through which those He created for <u>His benefit</u> *(increasing of His House)* and <u>pleasure</u> (to see the reflection of Himself – virtue - through Jesus Christ within those whom loved Him in Spirit and Truth) would be *saved* from their sins.

Jesus came in <u>*service*</u> of His Father, to <u>*fulfill*</u> all that God had already initiated from the beginning of time, *within* and *through* Himself. He walked on earth amongst His own people and they could not recognize Him as being the Messiah that they have been waiting for, for so long.

This brings to mind John 14:19, "*Yet a little while, and the world seeth me no more; but ye see me: because I live, ye shall live also*"... firstly, Jesus confirms here that He is now walking amongst them on earth and thus they can <u>see</u> Him, repent and accept His word as being from God as He speaks not of His own but in <u>servitude</u> <u>of His Father</u> (John 14: 24, "the word which ye hear is not mine, but the Father's which SENT me") but says He, shortly the world shall not be seeing Him anymore, and that refers to His *death and resurrection* and His ultimate *ascension* to heaven to *return* to His Father, in COMPLETION of His plan.

Those who saw Him in the flesh, were given it by God to recognize Him, for without God allowing it, they too would have remained blind. God brought His truth to the world through the Servant of His choosing, Himself. They who believed could SEE Him for whom He was, the Son of God, by the power of His grace, but they who only saw the fleshly body and persecuted Him for what He said in truth, they saw not beyond that which was given witnessed too through their sight (eyes).

WHO will be willing to deny himself the pleasure of his own will and passion, whilst suffering all kinds of humiliation, even unto death, when knowing one has the power to bring all subjects to oneself?

Who would stand in the remembrance of a plan that would ask the sacrifice of your own life, in exchange for the liberty and salvation of all those very people that in fact deny you, reject you, and sought to destroy and kill, what they fear as opposition to the self and what they have known to be true and correct?

What man would stand strong in seeing the end from the beginning and know the end would be death, even unto loving his persecutors?

Jesus Christ stood in one accord with His Father. He did not enter into reasoning discussions about the merit of giving up His life for the corrupted and defiled that were given to Him as His.

In John 18: 11, Jesus said to Simon Peter, after he smote the ear of the high priest's servant, one of those who came to arrest Him in Gethsemane, *"Put up thy sword into the sheath: the cup which my Father hath given me, shall I not drink it?"*....thus the Lord said: How can I not be captured and put to death, for all things have to be fulfilled in Me and through Me, so that you can live. I do the will of My Father and not the will of Myself nor that of any man. Hinder not them in whose power I have been placed, for now it's in their power to obtain power over Me, so all can be fulfilled as was prophesied of, for this is the will of My Father.

He accepted His responsibility as a servant to His Father. He came to bring truth and light, where error and darkness prevailed. He fulfilled the will of God, even when He knew His death in the flesh, would be the ransom to be paid.

He was found acceptable by God because of His obedience towards Him. He is the Son, in whom the Father is well pleased.

He is the Son whom the Holy Spirit bears witness to, because He is the plan of God for salvation.

In the Garden of Gethsemane, Luke 22: 42, Jesus prayed, saying, *"Father, if thou be willing, remove <u>this cup</u> (death) from me: nevertheless not <u>my</u> will, but <u>thine</u>, be done. (Subject to the will of God and not seeking His own will and pleasure)"*

And then, because of His obedience, resisting temptation of 'self pleasure' He overcame the self, as He stood in the plan(truth) of His Father, He was rewarded by God, sending forth an angel to appear to Him, by which He was strengthened so that he would endure all things to come in completion of the will of His Father. Thus, Luke 22: "And then appeared an angel unto him from heaven, strengthening him."

Jesus Christ is the hub of pure faith in God, without Him there would be no redemption and salvation. Salvation was designed with Jesus Christ as the plan and record for faith in mind, and thus Jesus fulfilled His obligation being the faithful obedient servant to the will of God and acting in the best interest of His Master.

Can ye see the importance of the obedient, faithful servant, in the building and sustaining of the house of his master; laboring to increase his master's house and not follow his own aspiration to build for himself??

Justifying the use of titles through application of scripture Many miss use scripture into saying what they want it to say. So, what does scripture say? Ephesians 4:10-14 (KJV)

"10 He that descended is the same also that ascended up far above all heavens, that he might fill all things.)

11 And he gave some, apostles; and some, prophets; and some, evangelists; and some, pastors and teachers;

12 For the <u>perfecting</u> of the saints, for the <u>work of the ministry</u>, for the <u>edifying of the body</u> of Christ:

13 Till we all come in the <u>unity of the faith,</u> and of the <u>knowledge of the Son of God</u>, unto a <u>perfect man,</u> unto the measure of the stature of the <u>fullness</u> of Christ:

14 That we henceforth be no more children, tossed to and fro, and carried about with every wind of doctrine, by the sleight of men, and cunning craftiness, whereby they lie in wait to deceive;" The question is: where does it say, give yourself a title?

Titles have become a symbol of honor and power and not of function in the church that detracts from the original purpose of <u>callings</u> authorized by God unto those He <u>elected</u> to be apostles, prophets, evangelists, teachers and pastors within His covenant.

God elects those who will function in each such a position (office) from the Body through the Holy Spirit. Each believer that is baptized with the Holy Spirit and is joined to Him in covenant, have been given a divine calling for function in the priesthood.

2 Thes 1:11

"Wherefore also we pray always for you, that our God would count you worthy of <u>this</u> calling, and fulfill all the good pleasure of his goodness, and the work of faith with power."

2 Pet 1:10

"Wherefore the rather, brethren, give diligence to make <u>your calling</u> and <u>election</u> <u>sure</u>: for if ye do these things, ye shall never fall."

Referring to Eph 4 vs. 12 *"For the <u>perfecting</u> of the saints, for the <u>work of the</u> <u>ministry</u>, for the <u>edifying of the body</u> of Christ:"* This is the reason for callings, none other and was given by God as a contact point (token) for faith within the Body. This is how our faith are made living, for in each calling is a certain measure of grace present that allows the office to fulfill the purpose given to them, through the authorized activity of faith (works of the Spirit) and this is also how we partake of Christ, being united as one over the bread of Christ and the oil of the Spirit. This is what God breathes into.

The elected office are called of grace by the Spirit of Truth to function in the office of His Church and are not selected and appointed by men <u>for</u> men in the churches raised up <u>by</u> men to honor religious leaders using the Name of our Lord, as they claim a title befitting their position in man-made churches. Callings are spiritual contact points by which the church is built in faith and growth. In denominational churches, the focus is on the charismatic leaders and their ability to connect to the congregation on the issues of life.

So, asking the same question….where is it written that each one that claims to be of the Spirit and minister the gospel may claim unto them a title of their own choosing??

The reason for this question is, that many religious people, form their own denominational church/ministry/group or splinter group from another denominational church and then claim a title according to the doctrine they embrace or denomination they belong too i.e. some apostles, prophets, evangelists, teachers and pastors. They claim representation of God by the title they adorn. A certain mindset and perception have developed in those who carry these unauthorized titles.

The *original intent* for these appointed and elected callings in the early church, was to establish a *government* for the church (the Body) of Jesus Christ in which each of these callings, had been allocated with a specified *function* (job description if you wish) and a certain measure of Grace from God (power), to fulfill the purpose of perfecting the saints, edification of the body and for the work of the ministry. This was *the government* of Jesus Christ that rested upon His shoulders, under *His stewardship*, being the High Priest of His Priesthood. In the absence of Jesus (physically), after His ascension, The Apostle Peter was the (physical) representative (the rock) of Jesus Christ including the appointed apostles, prophets, evangelists, teachers and pastors, through whom the truth of Jesus Christ was given to the Body, by the revelation of grace. Jesus Christ rules over His church spiritually as He is a Spirit. It was their appointed responsibility to function in their callings and therefore see to the growth of the saints of the Lord. Through their activity of faith, by which they got to know God, communicated with Him and fellowship with Him, in a *specified* way that was *taught* to them under *instruction of the apostles*.

This is nothing strange, as the Levitical Priesthood of the Israelites, followed specified cleansing and purifying laws, sacrificial laws and were given the structure of the temple in height, width, length and breadth including all the tokens/articles that were to be used and represented in the temple, that had to be handled or observed during their priesthood activity of faith. All of these things pointed to Jesus Christ and His redemptive work, - in part and was fulfilled in and through Him in His Spiritual Covenant.

For these callings to be fruitful in its original purpose, it has to be joined to His spiritual covenant, observing Jesus Christ in word and deed, in Spirit and in Truth, according to the terms set by God for pure faith.

Therefore a religious man cannot claim something (a title) whilst remaining outside the boundaries of God's covenant, as it is of <u>no</u> <u>effect</u>. Its purpose (callings) was designed for use within Covenant. It's here where the power of God is manifested unto those whom have to feed His sheep (Body), steward His knowledge (evangelize the truth to the unsaved/edify the Body) and perfect the saints (priesthood) in their responsibility towards God by observing His terms for salvation.

Also, confusion is in the order of the day, pertaining to what the purpose of callings are and have been misapplied and are now being used to profit and honor men using these titles as a symbol of authority whilst appointing themselves into those callings.

The use of these "titles' do not automatically give one authority and a direct line to the Lord just because it is now claimed by men and written in the Bible.

It was not a symbol of status or exaltation above others, but in fact, those who carried these names of being appointed apostles, prophets, evangelists, teachers and pastors, were but mere servants of the Lord, fulfilling their activity of faith and the responsibility added unto them according to the calling, to function therein.

The "title" they carried only IDENTIFIED them to the Body as being elected and appointed by God for a specified PURPOSE.

God set order to and in His government structure.

The saints were humbled by grace as they grew in grace (unto increased fruit and faith) and understood the true purpose of the callings as given by the Lord and thus, the church was brought into UNITY, as it came into unity of the Spirit by being in agreement with God on His plan (one mind), serving Him in word and indeed, as they embrace one truth under one elected government under inspiration of the Holy Spirit.

Due to the Church being segregated in denominational off-cuts, there is no unity in the Body, no agreement on doctrine, and Christ has become subject to the whims and needs of men.

Callings have become "Titles" and with that, abuse of the Church has taken place through grievous wolves plundering the sheep as they are led as sheep to a slaughter being taught false doctrine and appointing themselves as stewards of God.

By claiming a title, the title bearer has been, through the traditions of men, endowed with "power" to plunder and abuse the flock of Christ, harvesting tithes to fund their lifestyles of splendor and opulence, whilst the flock is left hungry and thirsty, for there is no truth and no power in faith to be found in the church devoid of the true gospel and stewardship.

In conclusion, we can see that a title maketh not the man, a man of God, but a true servant of the Lord is in servitude of God, stewarding the truth as given by Jesus Christ under His inspiration and according to the structure He has determined and ordered for the growth and restoration of His Church through the first apostles of the early church.

Using scripture to justify the use of giving oneself a title of either apostle, prophet, evangelist, teacher or pastor, is abuse of the original purpose for these callings and speaks of believers not understanding the purpose for them, as the perception is created that by these names/titles the person is of a higher standing than the congregation. This is untrue.

In the assembly of the Lord, all are equal and the purpose for an assembly is for the growth of the Body in unity, being of the same mind, in one truth and one Spirit, as they share the truth of the gospel of salvation under stewardship of the government.

This is the true purpose and if any man should take what was given by the Lord and apply it any other way, then the Lords approval and acceptance is not in what is being presented, because it does not reflect His plan and purpose for the function of the Church in faith.

Jesus Christ was chosen by the Father, Not to ONE office only, but too many:

To be a King, High Priest, Prophet and Mediator of His covenant. *"Ye are my witnesses, saith the LORD, and my servant whom I have chosen,"*

Isaiah 43:10

Ye are my witnesses, saith the Lord, and my servant whom I have chosen: that ye may be furnished and fully <u>qualified</u> for the <u>great work</u> (appointed) him.

"I have laid help upon one that is mighty; I have exalted one chosen out of the people,"

- servant, appointed into this position, to save His people from death and sin.

To bring the gospel of salvation unto those whom He has been given by the Father.

- *"ye may <u>furnished</u> and fitly <u>qualified</u> for the <u>great</u> <u>work</u> (appointed) him."* – establishing His covenant within and through Himself, His redemptive work is seen within those who are divinely transformed from the old man unto the new man, as the new temperament(virtue) is birthed within those that function in His priesthood.

Psalms 89:19

"Then thou speakest in vision to thy holy one, and saidst, I have laid help upon one that is mighty; I have exalted one chosen out of the people."

Jesus Christ, as God's Servant, sought not his own glory. *"I honor my Father,"* We honor God through our activity of faith, following due process for transformation of the soul, to reflect the virtue of Jesus Christ, that is a new temperament born within those of faith, that reflects the temperament of God through Jesus Christ.

John 8:49

"Jesus answered, I am not a devil; but I honor my Father, and ye do dishonor me."

John 7:17 - 18

"17 If any man will do <u>his will</u>, he shall know of the doctrine, whether it be of God, or whether I speak of myself. He that speaketh of himself seeketh his own glory: but he that seeketh his glory that sent him, the same is true

"18 He that speaketh of himself seeketh his own glory: but he that seeketh his glory that sent him, the same is true, and no unrighteousness is in him."

Luke 22:42

"Saying, Father ... nevertheless not my will, but thine, be done," Jesus asked in prayer for the Lord to spare him the cup of death, but in remembrance of His Fathers plan, He yielded and submitted Himself to the will of His Father, who knoweth all things and are the author of Truth. John 12: 27

"Now my soul is troubled, and what shall I say? Father save me from this hour: but <u>for this cause</u> have I came unto this hour." Obedience to His Fathers will, for He knew the purpose of His birth as God in the flesh.

"But the Father which sent me, he gave me a commandment, what I should say and what I should speak," John 12:49, *"For I have not spoken of myself; but the Father which sent me, he gave me a <u>commandment</u>, what I should say, and what I should speak."*

"Even as I have kept my Father's commandments," John 15:10 *"If ye keep my commandments, ye shall abide in my love; even as I have kept my Father's commandments, and abide in his love."* God seeks not emotional expressions of love by those whom love Him, He seeks obedience through faith, for the heart is fickle and ever-changing according to circumstance, needs and issues, but through faith we express our love for God; that is the expression of love He seeks, because faith mirrors Jesus Christ perfectly.

A Servant <u>seeks</u> not his own glory, nor does his own will, but stands <u>in agreement</u> with the will of his master (or father) and seeks to honor his master/father through all he does.

A servant <u>doeth</u> everything that is commanded him, not being ashamed to acknowledge himself to be a Servant.

A Servant may at times <u>be sent</u> abroad to do business or carry out the wishes of his father/master, far from home, and is thereby exposed to many dangers, and great hardships.

A Servant that is faithful, take <u>delight in doing</u> his father's/master's business, preferring it above his own meat and drink, as did the Servant of Abraham, who would not eat nor drink before he had done his errand, Genesis 24:33, *"And there was set meat before him to eat: but he said, I will not eat, until I have told mine errand.* And he said, *Speak on.*

A Servant that is <u>faithful</u> will not go beyond his commission in anything, thus will do what is expected of him. Saith God to Moses, *"And look that thou make them after <u>their pattern</u>, which was shewed thee in the mount,"* Exodu 25:40, And look that thou make them after their pattern, which was shewed thee in the mount, thus, follow the specified instructions given and add nothing or leave nothing out. Follow the plan.

"Thus did Moses: according to all that the LORD commanded him, so did he" Exodus40:16, Thus did Moses: according to all that the Lord <u>commanded</u> him, so did he. Moses followed the commandment of God, as specified to him by God, being the faithful servant he walked in the council of the Lord, not seeking to use his imagination to alter that which was already perfect and authorized.

Jesus Christ came to fulfill the work of God within Himself, being the Mediator of those of faith before the Lord; He was sent on a journey, as far as it is from heaven to earth, to sojourn amongst His own who knew Him not and was thereby exposed to much difficulty, and great hardships, from both men and devils, suffering vulnerability, humiliation, and pain unto death.

He was persecuted from place to place, his life often in jeopardy; he had no place to lay his head; and was in the end betrayed by one of His chosen 12 and rejected by the Jews who pleaded for Him to be put to death.

Matthew 8:20, *"And Jesus saith unto him, The foxes have holes, and the birds of the air have nests; but the Son of man hath not where to lay his head."*

The Lord Christ was most faithful. "Though he was a Son, yet learned obedience by the things which he <u>suffered</u>," Hebrews

5:8, "Though he was a Son, yet learned obedience by the things which he suffered. "Jesus saith unto them, My meat is to do the will of him that sent me, and to finish his work,"

John 4:34, *"Jesus saith unto them, My meat is to do the will of him that sent me, and to finish his work"*

"I delight to do thy will, O my God," Psalms 40:8 *I delight to do thy will, O my God: yea, thy law is within my heart."* The Law of the Lord is written upon the table of the heart, as the old man is divinely transformed unto the new man. It becomes the new nature of the new man that walks in obedience to the will of God through obedience in faith, according to the tradition of truth.

"Wist ye not that I must be about my Father's business?" saying, don't you know I am here to not do My own will and good pleasure, but to follow the commandment given to Me? To be the Lamb slain for the sins of the world?

The Lord Jesus Christ hath an absolute right to a reward for his work's sake. His reward is those given to Him by His Father for whom He has died, so that through them, His kingdom could be increased eternally unto glory and honor of His Father. Though there is no merit or eternal reward for the works of the flesh, which believers do today functioning as unprofitable, unfaithful servants. For after they have done all they could in trying to appease the Lord with these works of contrition, their faith remains in vain; yet there is great merit and worth in what Jesus Christ did.

And the Father will give him wages; he shall have his wife (his Church), for whom he served above fourteen years; nay, *"I shall give thee the heathen for thine inheritance, and the uttermost parts of the earth for thy possession,"* Psalms 2:8 *"Ask of me, and I shall give thee the heathen for thine inheritance, and the uttermost parts of the earth for thy possession."*

Isaiah 52:13,

"Behold, *my servant shall deal prudently, he shall be exalted and extolled, and be very high,*" "*Therefore will I divide him a portion with the great, and he shall divide the spoil with the strong; because he hath poured out his soul unto death,*" Isaiah 53:12 "*Therefore will I divide him a portion with the great, and he shall divide the spoil with the strong; because he hath poured out his soul unto death: and he was numbered with the transgressors; and he bare the sin of many, and made intercession for the transgressors.*"

The lot of the Lord (Deut 32) is those who love Him through obedience in faith. Those upon whom righteousness are imputed and are justified by Jesus Christ. He who is the propitiation (1 John 4:10) for our sins, bearing the persecution of sinners, enduring humiliation, carrying His cross to the hill upon which He was erected for all to see unto death. But in all, He followed instruction and kept to the plan as given by His Father.

But we see Jesus, who for the suffering of death, crowned with glory and honor; that He by the grace of God should taste death for every man. Hebrews 2:9, "*But we see Jesus, who was made a little lower than the angels for the suffering of death, crowned with glory and honor; that he by the grace of God should taste death for every man.*"

The Lord Jesus Christ was subject to the frailty of flesh, when in the flesh, being born of flesh, in the form of a Servant, (at some time) unto fear.

"*Made under the law,*" Galatians 4:4, "*But when the fullness of the time was come, God sent forth his Son, made of a woman, made under the law,*" "*He was troubled in spirit,*" John 13:21, "*When Jesus had thus said, he was troubled in spirit, and testified, and said, Verily, verily, I say unto you, that one of you shall betray me..*" And was heard in that he feared, Hebrews 5:7,

"Who in the days of his flesh, when he had offered up prayers and supplications with strong crying and tears unto him that was able to save him from death, and was heard in that he feared;"

Jesus Christ, although a servant of God, is essentially ONE with the Father.

The Father, the Son and the Holy Spirit, are the one everlasting and eternal God. *"For there are three that bear record in heaven, the Father, the Word, and the Holy Ghost: and these three are one,"* 1 John 5:7, *"For there are three that bear record in heaven, the Father, the Word, and the Holy Ghost: and these three are one."* Jesus Christ, although He be called the Servant of God, yet is He His own beloved Son, and "heir of all things, by whom also He made the worlds," Hebrews 1:2 *"Hath in these last days spoken unto us by his Son, whom he hath appointed heir of all things, by whom also he made the worlds;"* There is none in heaven and earth that hath greater glory, stature, or privilege, conferred upon Him, than the Lord Jesus Christ.

Jesus Christ had no necessity of nature laid upon Him, to accept the lower place and office of a Servant. He was not forced to it, but since He and the Father are One, they stood in agreement of the plan of God, that Jesus the Lamb of God, will be slain for the sins of the world and by His blood establish a covenant of the Spirit between the world and God, unto salvation.

We may note from hence the wonderful condescension of Jesus Christ; there is nothing which sets forth His great abasement for our sakes more than this. Doth the Son of God, who is the Lord of heaven and earth, become a Servant!

"Who, being in the form of God, thought it not robbery to be equal with God: But made himself of no reputation, and took upon him the form of a servant," Philippians 2:6 *"Who, being in the form of God, thought it not robbery to be equal with God:*

7 But made himself of no reputation, and took upon him the form of a servant, and was made in the likeness of men:"

"For even the Son of man came not to be ministered unto, but to minister," Mark 10:45, "For even the Son of man came not to be ministered unto, but to minister, and to give his life a ransom for many."

But some may inquire, whose Servant is Christ?

He is God's Servant: "Behold my Servant,"

Matthew 12:18 "Behold my servant, whom I have chosen; my beloved, in whom my soul is well pleased: I will put my spirit upon him, and he shall shew judgment to the Gentiles."

He is His people's Servant: Minister of truth

Matthew 20:28, *"Even as the Son of man came not to be ministered unto, but to minister, and to give his life a ransom for many."*

Let us learn from Him, to humble ourselves, through submission to God's grace. "Let this mind be in you, which was also in Christ Jesus," Philippians 2:5

Shall the Lord become a Servant? And shall the Servant swell in pride and arrogance, and nothing content him but to be called lord; nay, and lord it over God's heritage, whose servants they ought to be, if they would be gospel ministers. Surely Christ abhors him who calls himself the Servant of servants; whilst at the same time he exalts himself above all that is called gods.

If the Lord Christ became a willing, humble, laborious, and faithful Servant for us, let us labor to be humble, faithful, and sincere Servants to Him: He hath fulfilled the hardest work through and in Himself. "For thou also hast wrought all our works in us," Isaiah 26:12 Lord, thou wilt ordain peace for us: for thou also hast wrought all our works in us.

Let us follow His example, and be Servants one to another: *"For I have given you an example, that ye should do as I have done to you,"* John 13:15

To be the servant of the Lord profiteth the soul as the nature of Christ is formed within the soul, unto death of the old man, as we are joined to God through Jesus Christ in servitude to Him. Paul seems to glory more in it, than in his being an Apostle: *"If any man serve me, let him follow me; and where I am, there shall also my servant be: if any man serve me, he will my Father honor,"* John 12:26.

This justly reproves such who are ashamed to be mere servants of Christ Jesus, and to hear reproach and infamy for His name's sake, seeing He hath not stuck to serve them in denying Himself, even to death on the Cross.

Jesus had many titles allocated to Him in the scriptures but He never gave Himself one.

Are the men and women of this world greater than JESUS?

I should think not.

Don't use one scripture to justify yourselves in adorning ye self with a title of honor to seek honor for the self. Follow Him in the tradition He Himself came to establish for faith.

Jesus of Nazareth says, *"For everyone who exalts himself shall be humbled, and he who humbles himself shall be exalted."* and *"But it shall not be so among you. But whoever desires to be great among you, let him be your servant. And whoever of you desires to become first, he shall be servant of all."* and *"I am the Good Shepherd... and they shall hear My voice, and there shall be one flock, and one Shepherd."*

Matthew 23:12 | Luke 14:11 | Mark 10:43-44 | John 10:11,16

Here are Jesus' TITLES

Chief Cornerstone: (Ephesians 2:20) – Jesus is the cornerstone of the building which is His church. He cements together Jew and Gentile, male and female—all saints from all ages and places into one structure built on faith in Him which is shared by all.

Firstborn over all creation: (Colossians 1:15) – Not the first thing God created, as some incorrectly claim, because verse 16 says all things were created through and for Christ. Rather, the meaning is that Christ occupies the rank and pre-eminence of the first-born over all things, that He sustains the most exalted rank in the universe; He is pre-eminent above all others; He is at the head of all things.

Head of the Church: (Ephesians 1:22; 4:15; 5:23) – Jesus Christ, not a king or a pope, is the only supreme, sovereign ruler of the Church—those for whom He died and who have placed their faith in Him alone for salvation.

Holy One: (Acts 3:14; Psalm 16:10) – Christ is holy, both in his divine and human nature, and the fountain of holiness to His people. By His death, we are made holy and pure before God.

Judge: (Acts 10:42; 2 Timothy 4:8) – The Lord Jesus was appointed by God to judge the world and to dispense the rewards of eternity.

King of kings and Lord of lords: (1 Timothy 6:15; Revelation 19:16) – Jesus has dominion over all authority on the earth, over all kings and rulers, and none can prevent Him from accomplishing His purposes. He directs them as He pleases.

Light of the World: (John 8:12) – Jesus came into a world darkened by sin and shed the light of life and truth through His work and His words. Those who trust in Him have their eyes opened by Him and walk in the light.

Prince of peace: (Isaiah 9:6) – Jesus came not to bring peace to the world as in the absence of war, but peace between God and man who were separated by sin. He died to reconcile sinners to a holy God.

Son of God: (Luke 1:35; John 1:49) – Jesus is the "only begotten of the Father"

(John 1:14). Used 42 times in the New Testament, "Son of God" affirms the deity of Christ.

Son of man: (John 5:27) – Used as a contrast to "Son of God" this phrase affirms the humanity of Christ which exists alongside His divinity.

Word: (John 1:1; 1 John 5:7-8) – The Word is the second Person of the triune God, who said it and it was done, who spoke all things out of nothing in the first creation, who was in the beginning with God the Father, and was God, and by whom all things were created.

Word of God: (Revelation 19:12-13) – This is the name given to Christ that is unknown to all but Himself. It denotes the mystery of His divine person.

Word of Life: (1 John 1:1) – Jesus not only spoke words that lead to eternal life, but according to this verse He is the very words of life, referring to the eternal life of joy and fulfillment which He provides. His word (truth) brings life to the soul that was dead in sin.

His position in the trinity Alpha and Omega: (Revelation 1:8; 22:13) – Jesus declared Himself to be the beginning and end of all things, a reference to no one but the true God. This statement of eternality could apply only to God. From out of Him began all things and unto Him all will return. Alpha is our origin and Omega is our destiny, we return from whence we originated.

Emmanuel: (Isaiah 9:6; Matthew 1:23) – Literally "God with us." Both Isaiah and Matthew affirm that the Christ who would be born in Bethlehem would be God Himself who came to earth in the form of a man to live among His people.

I Am: (John 8:58, with Exodus 3:14) – When Jesus ascribed to Himself this title, the Jews tried to stone Him for blasphemy. They understood that He was declaring Himself to be the eternal God, the unchanging Jehovah of the Old Testament.

Lord of All: (Acts 10:36) – Jesus is the sovereign ruler over the whole world and all things in it, of all the nations of the world, and particularly of the people of God's choosing, Gentiles as well as Jews.

True God: (1 John 5:20) – This is a direct assertion that Jesus, being the true God, is not only divine, but is the Divine. Since the Bible teaches there is only one God, this can only be describing His nature as part of the triune God.

His Work on earth Author and Perfecter of our Faith: (Hebrews 12:2) – Salvation is accomplished through the faith that is the gift of God (Ephesians 2:8-9) and Jesus is the founder of our faith and the finisher of it as well. From first to last, He is the source and sustainer of the faith that saves us.

Bread of Life: (John 6:35; 6:48) – Just as bread sustains life in the physical sense, Jesus is the Bread that gives and sustains eternal life. God provided manna in the wilderness to feed His people and He provided Jesus to give us eternal life through His body, broken for us.

Bridegroom: (Matthew 9:15) – The picture of Christ as the Bridegroom and the Church as His Bride reveals the special relationship we have with Him. We are bound to each other in a covenant of grace that cannot be broken.

Deliverer: (Romans 11:26) – Just as the Israelites needed God to deliver them from bondage to Egypt, so Christ is our Deliverer from the bondage of sin.

Good Shepherd: (John 10:11,14) – In Bible times, a good shepherd was willing to risk his own life to protect his sheep from predators. Jesus laid down His life for His sheep, and He cares for and nurtures and feeds us.

High Priest: (Hebrews 2:17) – The Jewish high priest entered the Temple once a year to make atonement for the sins of the people. The Lord Jesus performed that function for His people once for all at the cross.

Lamb of God: (John 1:29) – God's Law called for the sacrifice of a spotless, unblemished Lamb as an atonement for sin. Jesus became that Lamb led meekly to the slaughter, showing His patience in His sufferings and His readiness to die for His own.

Mediator: (1 Timothy 2:5) – A mediator is one who goes between two parties to reconcile them. Christ is the one and only Mediator who reconciles men and God. Praying to Mary or the saints is idolatry because it bypasses this most important role of Christ and ascribes the role of Mediator to another.

Rock: (1 Corinthians 10:4) – As life-giving water flowed from the rock Moses struck in the wilderness, Jesus is the Rock from which flows the living waters of eternal life. He is the Rock upon whom we build our spiritual houses, so that no storm can shake them.

Resurrection and Life: (John 11:25) – Embodied within Jesus is the means to resurrect sinners to eternal life, just as He was resurrected from the grave. Our sin is buried with Him and we are resurrected to walk in the newness of life.

Savior: (Matthew 1:21; Luke 2:11) – He saves His people by dying to redeem them, by giving the Holy Spirit to renew them by His power, by enabling them to overcome their spiritual enemies, by sustaining them in trials and in death, and by raising them up at the last day.

True Vine: (John 15:1) – The True Vine supplies all that the branches (believers) need to produce the fruit of the Spirit— the living water of salvation and nourishment from the Word.

Way, Truth, Life: (John 14:6) – Jesus is the only path to God, the only Truth in a world of lies, and the only true source of eternal life. He embodies all three in both a temporal and an eternal sense.

Jesus was all of these but yet He called Himself "a servant". How dare any man or woman give themselves titles. Follow the example set by JESUS according to His tradition of faith and not the traditions of men.

Be blessed brothers and sisters in Jesus' Mighty Name. Amen

The Key to Salvation:
Virtue = First Fruits of Christ

How many of you have heard the words "<u>virtue</u>" or "<u>virtuous</u>" and associated it with being *morally correct* and *behaving a certain way* and being a *certain type of person* that at times just doesn't feel right to one self, doesn't "gel" with who you are or want to be, generating feelings of uneasiness, discomfort, guilt, shame or maybe even feelings of longing to obtain it.

Trying to be morally correct and acceptable is a very trying exercise for most people, although it's a deep-seated desire to be accepted by others and to be a good person (godliness).

Of course many think that this exercise is really unobtainable and is only for those who are willing to "self sacrifice" their life by being separated from the things that men cleave to in the world, therefore many shy away from becoming true followers of Jesus Christ, as they are not willing to leave behind what they hold dear to the self or let go of who they have worked so hard to become willingly or through the toils, snares and hardships of living in a world of death and suffering.

General perceptions that cause stumbling-blocks, to name but a few, is either that when you become a Christian, you are impoverished and have a life of loss and lack, or others might perceive that you can't enjoy your life anymore and have to walk around solemnly devoid of any joy, and/or then of course you also have those whom boast that they are the Lords favorites and His "unmerited" favor rests upon them of which they can show the evidence of the "full barn" (financial security) they have acquired...so there are many misconceptions in the minds of men built from the foundation and impact of the socio-economic group, gender, race and religious – and family traditions they find themselves born into that begets prejudice based on our life experiences.

Whatever the perception, it's a stumbling block to those who love themselves more than what they love God and are seeking reasons for not embracing God in truth, thus resisting the Hand of the Lord, as it seems like real hard work, whilst others perceive through their education with the religious traditions/doctrine of men, that there are no work involved at all, that salvation is received when one repent and confess faith in God through Jesus Christ, not understanding the following - that although salvation is freely attainable by all of mankind through the sacrifice of the Lamb for the sins of the world, not all of mankind are willing to accept the gift of salvation on God's terms and partake of the subsequent labor of faith needed in order to obtain salvation through Jesus Christ, whilst carrying the yoke of His Death and Resurrection(cross). An *activity of faith* is needed for man's salvation to be complete in Jesus Christ, that requires denying the self(dying daily) of the things that are most common to man(flesh: knowledge of the world, wisdom of the world) to obtain the things from Above through obedience in faith doing righteousness(serve God in word and in deed) in a sanctified priesthood, through *due process* that brings forth *divine transformation* (regeneration) by *divine power*, of the soul: from being of the *flesh*(natural man/old man) to being of the *Spirit*(spiritual man/new man). Therefore, salvation is through Jesus Christ yes, but salvation requires <u>participation of faith</u>. God *designed* salvation with participation in mind, which means, there is *an activity* involved – an activity has to take place - that is a requirement for faith to be *empowered and fruitful* and for salvation to be ensured. Without the ACTIVITY, there will be NO divine TRANSFORMATION which means, no purging, cleansing and healing of the soul to take on the Life of Christ Jesus within.

Romans 12:2

"And be not <u>conformed</u> to this world: but <u>*be ye transformed*</u> by <u>*the renewing of your mind,*</u> that ye may prove what is that good, and acceptable, and perfect, will of God."

Do not embrace the knowledge of this world by which ye are put to sleep: When man accepts and uphold the knowledge of this world, it becomes the standard (your own standard) by which evidence is given to faith: such as good works of the flesh, the keeping of the 10 commandments, observing of water, wine and foot washings, song services etc. These are *carnal contact points* for faith not authorized by God for His spiritual covenant, and not spiritual contact points as given through Jesus Christ. Through these carnal contact points, believers try to pay tribute to Jesus Christ, but due to them not being authorized for contact with God, there is NO divine contact, NO divine change through the operation of God (regeneration) and thus, NO effectual working of the Holy Spirit. In Col 2:22 we read, "Which all are to <u>perish</u> with the using; after the <u>commandments and doctrine of men?</u>"

<u>Those of the Spirit,</u> *conform* to the knowledge of Jesus Christ through their consistency in studying the doctrine of truth that brings us in harmony with God, by touching Christ with the tokens of their priesthood.

We "conform" when we acknowledge, mold with and submit to the knowledge of Jesus Christ by using the tokens of labor, through the effective working power of the Spirit.

This is also the working of conformity that takes place with the labor of false knowledge – to acknowledge, mold with and submit to the knowledge of the world, through the power of the Antichrist. Similar operation, different knowledge, different spirit, different fruit born within.

- *be ye transformed* - from flesh to Spirit - divine transformation from flesh to spirit through activity of faith, by the effectual working power of the Spirit.

- *the renewing of your mind* - receiving the perspective of Jesus Christ = being of the same mind: through regeneration the senses are re-educated and that is what happens to the mind too, its re-educated by the power of grace and truth; as we conform to His truth, the imagery of the mind (Satan works with imagery) is transformed to see Christ clearly in truth and so we are in one mind with Him, we have His perspective and are thus like-minded.

We have His perspective when we see His plan clearly before us as we gain understanding of His plan through the process of regeneration.

The carnal mind works with false knowledge but the spiritual mind, with holy knowledge and thus thinking patterns change from what the mind was inclined to labor with, to now reflect on His knowledge and place all thoughts on the scale of truth, discerning error from truth, darkness from light, death from life. This is the renewing of the mind. When the mind changes the substance (knowledge) it labor with, then the soul is transformed by the impact of truth within.

2 Cor 4:16

"For which cause we faint not; but though our outward man (old man) perishes (death through transformation), yet the inward man (new man) is renewed (resurrected) day by day (due process of transformation through cycles of growth - testing)."

The moral code is not virtue – there is a difference between goodness of character and divine virtue

Did you know that the _moral center_ governs acceptable behavior within communities and sets a pattern of rebuke, chastisement and judgment, so all would conform to one acceptable standard by the acceptable principles (law) of those that govern the immediate communities, towns, cities and countries? Transgression of the moral laws is enforced and punishable by the law of man.

In Romans 2:15 Apostle Paul wrote about the moral code/center, _"Which shew the work of the law written in their hearts, their conscience also bearing witness, and their thoughts the mean while accusing and excusing one another."_

God is a God of love, kindness, forgiveness, goodness and strength; all of these attributes are present in man; His characteristics being set in us do not make us like Him. These things speak of the moral code, which God imprinted as _a memorial_ of Himself within each heart, as He imprinted the _moral code upon the soul_. So, we too have these characteristics, because it is begotten of God as He created Adamites in His image.

The moral code is a design of the Law of Moses, but where the Law of Moses was imprinted on rock, so the moral code was imprinted upon the soul. The moral code acts as a <u>law</u> that is <u>written in</u> our hearts, by which we know not to covet, steal, kill or lie and to love our neighbor. We just <u>know</u> this is wrong in the first and good to do in the last (love thy neighbor), thus, <u>written/imprinted in the heart</u>. Can you see?

We know it's wrong or right (i.e. love thy neighbor) and this is the imprint of the moral code that governs our behavior. Thus God has set _within_ us, a _governing factor_ called the _moral code_, by which our _conduct is regulated_ in order for us to not _offend_ one another. This is evident when observing the various religions and philosophies of the world, which all center on the _same_ moral code.

As the moral code passes through the filter of education, religion, tradition, gender, culture and philosophies *the moral center* is produced, embraced and enforced.

The *<u>the moral center</u> is evident in the conversations of people, pertaining to their moral goodness, kindness, honesty, purity, family values and weighing right from wrong, even world peace or defending issues they feel strongly about. Listen to the conversation around you. The moral code is the scale for determining what is wrong/right, acceptable/unacceptable; assumptions and presumptions are generated based upon past experiences in life, that will be taken as evidence against and of a preconceived judgment for an offense done against you/another by an offender of your own law (principles). The moral code is the law of the self that becomes the basis of your PRINCIPLES that you adopt, by which YOU live, it's your own PERSONAL LAW. It's the law by which you judge others and weigh circumstances to be acceptable or not.

Now, the reason I speak about the moral center/code, is because people are *inclined* to feel that because they know *these* things are part of God's character, it entitles them to automatically use these to *connect* to God on His level of faith. The same can be said about our unique signature *gifts and talents*, all begotten of God yes, but definitely not to be utilized to connect with God.

Virtue – 1. Moral goodness; a particular form of this i.e. honesty is a virtue

Virtue – 2. A good quality, an advantage i.e. the cars main virtue is its economy

Virtuous (adjective) virtuously (adverb)

Now, looking down below, at the summary of what is said to be virtue, it can be *observed* that it all speaks of a *good character*, of *goodness*, portraying certain *qualities* that is highly acceptable, of being of *sound moral standard*. Look carefully and keep them in mind as we proceed forth in explaining to you the difference between being of good character and being filled with virtue that is heaven bound, holy, unfeigned, a transformation *within* that is expressed *outwardly*.

- *Goodness, virtuousness, righteousness, morality, ethicalness, uprightness, Upstandingness, integrity, dignity, rectitude, honesty, honourableness, honourability, Honour, incorruptibility, probity, propriety, decency, respectability, nobility, nobility of soul/spirit, nobleness, worthiness, worth, good, trustworthiness, meritoriousness, Irreproachable Ness, blamelessness, purity, pureness, lack of corruption, merit, principles, high principles*

Adamites feel the spark of divinity of being destined for greater things, but that's all it is, a spark of recognition, a knowing that we are not destined for *death and suffering* but for much more, for a *greater destiny*, which by the way, man aspires to by living out his unique strengths - talents and gifts given to him by God for fulfillment and joy of his life on earth and striving for completion by these through his imagination, resourcing his own principles to establish a memorial to himself – a legacy – on earth in his lifetime. Even if he reaches the pinnacle of ambition, he will still feel incomplete and that's because he is NOT complete, for completion of the soul is only in and through Jesus Christ, as was proposed by God. The soul was designed to be completed in and through Jesus Christ, nothing else.

We <u>can not</u> obtain godliness (doing right), holiness, peace or fulfillment/completion by the moral code. (Yes, no matter HOW hard you try.) The <u>purpose</u> for the imprint of the moral code upon the soul is to *establish social equity that keeps society from anarchy*.

Can you see the necessity for this and how great God's wisdom is, to set within each heart a governing factor that regulates behavior, to a conforming of acceptable behavior, in order for Adamites to live relatively 'peaceable' and ordered lives?

It's an assumption made, that we can serve and worship God by the moral code (self) or moral center – just because we have the same characteristics as God has. There is a definite difference between *virtue as the fruits of the Spirit* and *virtue pertaining to goodness of character* through attaining a certain stature of behavior through the moral code.

The ONLY way we can connect with God, is through Jesus Christ, our contact point for faith in His Spiritual Covenant, and the door through which we *have* to enter to be received of and found acceptable and worthy of by God, as He engrafts the Holy Spirit within those who believe, through the "Baptism of the Holy Spirit".

Our completion is IN and THROUGH Jesus Christ only.

Col.2:10 *"And you are complete in him (Jesus), which is the head of all principality and power"*

Virtue

Virtue = JESUS CHRIST

Virtue = Grace (Power of God)

Virtue = Fruits of the Spirit (Temperament of Jesus)

Thus: Virtue = Grace + Fruits of the Spirit = power + glory of God = Jesus Christ Therefore: by the virtue birthed within the soul, the obedient and faithful (righteous) are called Sons of God, through the adoption of the Spirit.

Virtue is the power of God in the soul that reflects the image of Christ Jesus, as grace is the power of God; therefore grace is also virtue, for it brings healing, purging and cleansing of the soul to take on the likeness of Christ.

Power of God = virtue.

True virtue is the power of God manifested in the soul that reflects Jesus Christ perfectly. Therefore the Father says, 'In them I am well pleased, because I see My Son in them'. When God sees His Son in the soul, He sees a mirror image of Himself, because the Father and the Son are One. This is pleasing to Him.

By the *birth of virtue* (= the birth of Jesus Christ within the soul) through the *process of regeneration and renewing of the mind*, the soul takes on the likeness of Jesus Christ, who is the Son of God and God Himself.

The only *acceptable image* God finds pleasing, is *His own Image* within the souls of the obedient consenters to His plan for salvation through Jesus Christ. For by consenting (being in agreement) to His plan, the faithful walk <u>in righteousness</u>, as they follow the prophetic path as laid out in the Bible from Genesis onward to the last book as written under His Inspiration (Holy Spirit) and revealed by grace regarding His plan for salvation and how to receive it..

True righteousness is meeting the standard of God, for acceptance by Him.

What is God's standard?

- Jesus Christ. He is our righteousness.

When do we meet God's standard?

- When we ABIDE in His righteousness and His righteousness is Jesus Christ.

Thus, when we abide in Jesus Christ righteousness is imputed (declared), because we *obey* the call of grace to be joined to Him. We obey when we *respond* to His grace (call) in faith. <u>Then</u> we are obedient. (Rom 8:4) When do we abide in Jesus Chris?

- Through our activity of faith with the tokens/spiritual contact points for faith, as sanctified by God, for faith's expression. When we labor with His knowledge and tokens, we abide in Him.

When we know the righteousness of God, we are *set free* (justified) (Rom 8:2) from all the different belief systems, options to faith and merged solutions using the knowledge of the world, that's used by Adam to make Adam acceptable to God by His own measure.

When the standard of God is met, THEN the believer through continual practise of faiths labor is in *right-standing* with God and *enmity* is removed between God and man. This is when God says, "you are My friend'

Rom 3:22 says, *"even the <u>righteousness of God</u> which is <u>by faith</u> of Jesus Christ unto all and upon all them that believe: for there is no difference"*

Eph 2:15 *"Having abolished in his flesh the <u>enmity</u>, even the law of commandments contained in ordinances (*law of Moses: 10 commandments, the law that accuse and condemn the sinful nature of man*); for to make <u>in himself</u> of twain <u>one new man</u> (*divine transformation =>virtue*) so making <u>peace</u>"*(we are at peace with God and the enmity is removed)

Rom 8:2 *"For the law of the Spirit of life* (law of grace and truth*) in Christ Jesus hath made me <u>free</u> from the law of sin and death* (law of Moses*)"*

Rom 8:4 *"That <u>the righteousness</u> of the law (law of grace and truth) might <u>be fulfilled</u> (birth of new man: spiritual man)) in us, who walk not after the flesh but <u>after the Spirit</u>."*

Rom 8:7 "the <u>*carnal mind is enmity against God*</u>: *for it's not subject to the law of God, neither indeed can be."*(The carnal mind follows his own law and is independent from God, walking in the traditions of man, forming himself into a man of his own desire)

When the First Adam fell from grace, he became the son of Satan. This means that Satan was given the power by God to rule over Adam from that day hence. Satan rules the atmosphere, Adam rules over the earth. Adam chose to listen to Satan's council in the Garden of Eden by which he fell.

Satan is "the prince of the air", the antichrist spirit, as we read in 1 John 4:3, *"And every spirit that confesses not that Jesus Christ is come in the flesh is not of God: and this is that spirit of antichrist, whereof ye have heard that it shall come; and even now already is it in the world,"*

…..with the result that his influence is invisible to the eye but nonetheless is a living presence and reality. He influences the minds and hearts of men, to walk contrary to God, to walk independent of God, to walk in their own council, to distrust God, to seek resolution for all contradictions by the principle and aspiration empowered by the imagination of man, they seek to build their own kingdom rather than the kingdom of God, they seeks to rule, dominate and destroy by their own standard (own law) rather than to lay down the *<u>idols of the heart</u>* before the altar of Jesus Christ and be subject to the Spirit of truth by grace. This is the reality of being subject to Satan's system of sin of which the fruits are called iniquity, which have deep roots in the soul.

Idols of the heart are anything that man place above God, anything that man chooses to do or follow that takes him away from God. Those which become the mold of one's perception and consequently the affections of the heart and thus, let him stumble to walk in his own power and follow his own purpose for life. Did you know that <u>God created Adam with one purpose in mind</u>, and that was to establish for Himself, through the seed of Adam, an eternal kingdom whereby the seed of Adam would be the inheritors to His throne and all He created in His kingdom. God created us with the purpose of making a people for Himself, but our purpose on earth is to increase with virtue and to steward His grace, thus loving our neighbor like we do ourselves and so be found worthy and acceptable for our return Home.

The reality created by Satan for all mankind is the *system* we have been embracing and following since our birth into sin and death. Our minds have been taught to resource false knowledge, not because we wanted to, but because we are born into sin and death. And that was our education. The soul is scarred by our contact with false knowledge. We have been put to sleep, to not 'see' the truth through which we will get to know God the way He intended us to know Him, and that is by grace and truth. Truth is the ointment that heals the soul.

Everything we labor with that does not *confirm* Jesus Christ and does not *tether* us to God, *rooting* us in Jesus, is *not of* God, and is *contrary to truth*, which makes it *false*. Can you see that?

The reality Satan painstakingly designed, initiated and implemented is the system of false knowledge, the false reality, under which all Adamites fall, as it sympathizes with our human frailty, and the pain and suffering we endure in this world. It sympathizes with those things that's common to man (the flesh). Satan will never lead anyone to the truth of God, but has designed many options for faith that have been embraced by men in the form of traditions (culture and religious) and philosophies through which Adamites have tried to connect with God to no avail. The soul of man has taken on the image of Satan, and that is the image God sees when he looks into the soul: The image of sin and death. His desire is for us to mirror Him and be like Him inwardly (soul with virtue) and express Him outwardly (charity – expressing Christ in words called spiritual sacrifices of prophecy that confirms Jesus Christ) as we are transformed from the old unto the new. Then we are worthy and acceptable and He is well pleased.

THIS is the Virtue of Christ being formed within the righteous that is the temperament of Jesus Christ and the substance of Him that makes the soul acceptable to God. For nothing man can enter into the substance of Christ.

Gal 5:22 – 23, *"but the fruit of the Spirit is love, joy, peace, longsuffering, gentleness, goodness, faith, meekness, temperance: against such there is no law."*

Rom 8:23, *"And not only they, but ourselves also, which have the firstfruits of the Spirit..."*

1 Cor 15:20, *"But now is Christ risen from the dead, and become the firstfruits of them that slept."*

Eph 5:9 – 10, *"(For the fruit of the spirit is in all goodness and righteousness and truth;) Proving what is ACCEPTABLE to the Lord,"*

JESUS CHRIST BORN OF A VIRGIN WAS ALSO PURE.

Virgin 1: a person, specially a woman, who has never been defiled through intimacy with a man

Virgin 2: of a virgin; spotless; not yet touched (oxford)

Thus: Virginity (undefiled and uncorrupted, pure) = Virtue

(undefiled and uncorrupted, pure)

To be virginal is to be untouched and undefiled.

To be a virgin is to not have experienced mating in the flesh. Keep this in mind as we proceed forth from here.

It's amazing to see how God has set that in practise in faith, keeping faith pure and undefiled within a system (truth) into which Satan cannot enter because Gods contact point for faith (Jesus Christ) is undefiled and pure and the terms for faith is in Him not in anything that is of the world. So he cannot corrupt it and he cannot defile it because it is set within boundaries (framework of truth) that require re-education to truth from false knowledge (SYSTEM OF SIN) and being actively involved in working out one's own salvation through labor with His knowledge and tokens, by which one is separated from the world unto Him, through which the soul remains pure and undefiled.

God designed the soul to increase with knowledge. So the kingdom one embraces is the knowledge one conforms to: Either truth or err; Light or darkness under inspiration of the power of that kingdom, the Holy Spirit or the Antichrist spirit. For the soul to return unto pureness and an undefiled state, the consciousness is made pure by contact with truth. Jesus is the door of our consciousness and when our consciousness is pure so our soul is healed through our contact with Him, as we touch Him with the tokens He provided for our purging, cleansing and healing within.

Reading Luke 1:27-35 (KJV), *"To a virgin espoused to a man whose name was Joseph, of the house of David; and the virgin's name was Mary. And the angel came in unto her, and said, Hail, thou that art highly favored, the Lord is with thee: blessed art thou among women. And when she saw him, she was troubled by what he said, and cast in her mind what manner of salutation this should be. And the angel said unto her, Fear not, Mary: for thou hast found favor with God. And, behold, thou shalt conceive in thy womb, and bring forth a son, and shall call his name*

JESUS. He shall be great, and shall be called the Son of the Highest: and the Lord God shall give unto him the throne of his father David: And he shall reign over the house of Jacob forever; and of his kingdom there shall be no end. Then said Mary unto the angel, <u>How shall this be, seeing I know not a man?</u> And the angel answered and said unto her, <u>The Holy Ghost</u> shall come upon thee, and <u>the power of the Highest shall overshadow</u> thee: therefore also that <u>holy thing which shall be born of thee</u> shall be <u>called the Son of God.</u>"

Mary, mother of Jesus was chosen by God to bear His Son. He chose a virgin that was untouched and undefiled. She knew not the touch of a man (flesh). The passion of the flesh outside the bonds of marriage corrupts and leads the mind and emotions astray to seek the pleasure of the flesh without responsibility or perceived consequence. That is likened to the kingdom of darkness.

It is edifying to see how this event points to Jesus Christ as divinely born by mating of the Holy Ghost with a young virgin(untouched/ undefiled/pure/spotless), symbolizing the Lord as the husband and the Church being the pure and spotless bride, awaiting the mating with her husband for the increase of His House.

Mary knew not the lust of the flesh, she was still pure in mind and in body, untouched by lustfulness and this speaks to the Bride of Christ being brought to that state (through regeneration and renewing of the mind) in order for the mating to take place, for the increase of His House, His kingdom, whereby all the fruit born from that union will be of Him and a testimony to Him in glory and power.

The event symbolizes the union between God (through Jesus Christ) with His Bride. That's why God chose a virgin, as she knew not the power of the flesh (lust of flesh) but was untouched by that which corrupts and defiles (the passion of man/emotions/

imagery), so that the fruit born from her womb would be pure, untouched by man and thus speaks of divine power (power unto glory).

Jesus was born through mating of the Spirit with the pure and undefiled bride. Those of the Spirit are reborn through engraving of the Spirit within and the fruit (virtue) born within the soul, is divine fruit (virtue) as it is the mirror image of the substance (temperament) of Jesus Christ by which the soul is known to be of God.

As Jesus was born of a pure womb by the power of the Holy Spirit, so we too are also reborn of a pure womb (truth) by the power of the Spirit. The fruit of the union between the virgin and the Holy Ghost is Jesus Christ; the fruit born within the soul through mating with the Holy Ghost is a virtue that is Jesus Christ.

Virtue is the substance of Jesus that is the power of God.

Virtue as the first fruits of the Spirit is *divine*, formed through *divine power* that speaks of a divine transformation of the soul and by that substance those of the Spirit, are given the title of being called "Sons of God".

Virtue as the first fruits of the Spirit is the temperament of Christ formed within the soul through fruit-bearing unto virtue that mirrors/reflects Him perfectly.

- 1 John 3:1 reads, "What manner of love the Father hath bestowed upon us, that we should be *called the sons of God*:

therefore the world knoweth us not, because it knows him not."

- Gal 4:19, "...until Christ be formed in you."

Luke 8:43-48 (KJV) *"And a woman having an issue of blood"*
"43. And a woman having an issue of blood twelve years, which had spent all her living upon physicians, neither could be healed of any,

44. Came behind him, and touched the border of his garment: and immediately her issue of blood stanched.

45. And Jesus said, Who touched me? When all denied, Peter and they that were with him said, Master, the multitude throng thee and press thee, and sayest thou, Who touched me?

46. And Jesus said, Somebody <u>hath touched me</u>: for I perceive <u>that virtue is gone out of me.</u>

47. And when the woman saw that she was not hiding, she came trembling, and falling down before him, she declared unto him before all the people <u>for what cause she had touched him, and how</u> she was healed immediately.

48. And he said unto her, Daughter, be of good comfort: <u>thy faith hath made thee whole; go in peace."</u>

Verse 46: look at what JESUS said, *"Somebody <u>hath touched me</u>: for I perceive <u>that virtue is gone out of me."</u>*

The woman was afflicted for many years by an illness that made her very sick, and no cure of man was to be found. The knowledge of physicians (*knowledge of the world*) was not at power to bring healing to her (*no power in death and sin unto life*). The aspirations of the doctors by their education (*education of false knowledge*) was to bring healing (*false gospels of Christ in denominations*) but it had no effect, she remained sick *(condition of the church today)*. She had faith in her heart (*impact of grace unto righteousness, for she believed*). If she didn't have faith, she would not willingly have followed <u>through</u> on her next action:

She then acted on her faith, she TOUCHED (activity of faith) Jesus Christ in faith.

At that moment, in the presence of her faith and by her ACTIVITY OF FAITH (labor of knowledge and tokens), Jesus felt VIRTUE leave Him. He felt His POWER leave Him. There was an exchange taking place to bring forth a change in her. She received that power and when it impacted (penetrated her body) her body she was healed from her illness.. Jesus Christ was her contact point for faith. Through Him and by touching (labor of faith) Him, she was healed. She was joined to Him through faith.

For healing to be initiated by the power of God, faith has to present and for the process to affect a change, an activity is needed, an activity of faith, which brings the process full circle.

This speaks of our salvation through Jesus Christ. For the soul to be healed, purged and cleansed (new man), faith has to be present and an activity of faith (works of the Spirit) to be followed through to carry forward the process of regeneration that takes place within the soul. Through the process of regeneration the fruits of the Spirit are born within, that is the power of God within the soul, to bring forth the mirror image of Him within that is the mirror image of Jesus Christ. By this power (virtue) we are found acceptable of the Lord, as it is

His power (virtue) that resembles Him is evident in the soul.

Therefore, an exchange has to take place, where God initiates grace and we respond in faith, for regeneration to take place through due process.

Can you see this?

The virtue of Jesus that left Him is the power of God that affects change and the power of God is in His virtue, and the virtue (fruits) of the Spirit is Jesus Christ formed within the soul. Wow!

The virtue He felt leaving Him is the power of God in Him. The woman was physically healed from a fleshly illness of the body. But when the power of God brings healing to the soul, the effect of that healing cannot be seen by the eye, but is evident through the actions of the one in whom the fruit is born, his/her response in times of contradiction when the heat of an offense is at its highest. The Lord issues His peace for the heart to endure the cutting away (circumcision) of the fruit of iniquity in the heart during the process of regeneration as the emotions are subdued in the presence of His peace, and the soul finds its rest from laboring with the knowledge of sin (knowledge of the world).

We touch Jesus Christ in His spiritual covenant when we labor with His knowledge and tokens for faith's activity, doing works of the Spirit, the new man is born from the ashes of the old man, to take on the image of Jesus Christ within. To touch Him we need an activity of faith, which is our labor of faith with the tokens He provided, doing righteousness. When we touch Him, we are joined to Him and this is the intent of God, that we shall increase with fruit through our contact with Jesus, have the experience with Christ's virtue and so increase in His kingdom.

<u>Luke 6: 17 – 20 (KJV)</u>" *there went virtue out of him*"

"17 And he came down with them, and stood in the plain, and the company of his disciples, and a great multitude of people out of all Judaea and Jerusalem, and from the sea coast of Tyre and Sidon, which came to hear him, and to be healed of their diseases; 18 And they that were vexed with unclean spirits: and they were healed.

19 And the whole multitude <u>sought to touch him: for there went virtue out of him, and healed them all.</u>

20 And he lifted up his eyes on his disciples, and said, Blessed be ye poor: for yours is the kingdom of God.

Verse 19: *the whole multitude <u>sought to touch him: for there went virtue out of him, and healed them all.</u>*

Once again as with the woman, we see here that the reputation of Jesus preceded Him and the multitudes flocked to Him, being called by grace, they responded in faith (grace reveals Jesus Christ and draws faith from the heart) an activity had to take place in order for them to be healed from their infirmities. They had to TOUCH Him. He was their contact point for faith). At their touch, His virtue left Him and they were healed.

This points to how the souls are healed through the response of faith to grace and an activity of faith taking place, with Jesus Christ being the contact point for faith, in order for the soul to take on the mirror image of Jesus Christ by the virtue born within.

<u>2 Peter 1:1- 20(KJV)</u> 'Virtue is the reward for faiths labor, without virtue we won't be accepted by the Lord'

1 Simon Peter, a servant and an apostle of Jesus Christ, to them that have obtained like precious <u>faith with us through the righteousness</u> <u>of God</u> and our Saviour Jesus Christ:

2 Grace and peace be multiplied unto you through the knowledge of God, and of Jesus our Lord,

3 According as his <u>divine power</u> hath given unto us all things that pertain unto life and godliness, through <u>the knowledge of him</u> that hath called us to <u>glory and virtue</u>:

4 Whereby are given unto us exceeding great and precious promises: that by these ye might be <u>partakers of the divine nature</u>, having escaped the <u>corruption that is in</u> <u>the world through lust.</u>

5 And beside this, giving all diligence, <u>add to your faith virtue</u>; and to <u>virtue knowledge;</u>

6 And to knowledge temperance; and to temperance patience; and to patience godliness;

7 And to godliness brotherly kindness; and to brotherly kindness charity.

8 For if these things be in you, and abound, they make you that ye shall neither be <u>barren nor unfruitful in the knowledge of our Lord Jesus Christ</u>.

9 But he that lacketh these things is <u>blind, and cannot see afar off</u>, and hath forgotten that he was <u>purged from his old sins</u>.

10 Wherefore the rather, brethren, give diligence to make your calling and election sure: for if ye do these things, ye shall never fall:

11 For so an <u>entrance shall be ministered</u> unto you abundantly into the everlasting kingdom of our Lord and Saviour Jesus Christ."

Verse 3: by the power of God the soul is transformed to be of a divine nature that is the nature of Jesus Christ. This is the virtue of Jesus Christ within that is the new life born of the Spirit. The fruits of the Spirit are the glory of the Lord as it is of His substance and thereby we glorify the Lord.

The crowning glory of God is Jesus Christ within the soul.

The only way we can become as He is, is by conforming to His knowledge through our diligent labor with His truth, touching Him daily through our labor with His spiritual tokens of faith as the mind are re-educated unto truth and freed from false knowledge.

Verse 5: The end product of faith is virtue as the living evidence of Christ within the soul, expressed through the behavior and words spoken by the righteous. Virtue is the reward for faith's labor, without virtue we won't be accepted by the Lord.

Both kingdoms function with knowledge, both have the reward of fruit, but the one is an offense to God and the other is His glory.

By the fruit we bear, we reveal to the Lord that we are of Him and thus will be accepted of Him, found worthy in Christ who is the measure for faith.

Proverbs 31:10-20 (KJV) 'The Body of Christ glorified by virtue, glorifies the giver thereof'

10 Who can find a virtuous woman? for her price is far above rubies.

11 The heart of her husband doth safely trust in her, so that he shall have no need of spoil.

12 She will do him good and not evil all the days of her life. 13 She seeketh wool, and flax, and worketh willingly with her hands.

14 She is like the merchants' ships; she bringeth her food from afar. 15 She riseth also while it is yet night, and giveth meat to her household and a portion to her maidens.

16 She considereth a field, and buyeth it: with the fruit of her hands she planted a vineyard.

17 She girdeth her loins with strength, and strengtheneth her arms.

18 She perceived that her merchandise was good: her candle goeth not out by night.

19 She layeth her hands to the spindle, and her hands hold the distaff.

20 She stretcheth out her hand to the poor; yea, she reacheth forth her hands to the needy.

Look at verse 10: We must become virtuous men and women of GOD that can only be done through JESUS CHRIST as our contact point for faith.

The above can be likened to the Body of Christ, being full of virtue, laboring for the House of her husband, she seeks not her own interest or pleasure but abides in the pattern for life given to her, so that she will in due diligence labor for the glory of her husband, finding her strength and endurance in the labor she does daily as she carries the yoke of her labor in joy and consistency.

She feeds the family and takes care of her neighbor by the fruits of her labor. She builds her husband's house not forsaking her path she has chosen, bearing fruit to be a testimony to his power in her.

We glorify the Lord as the giver of life when we bear fruit unto virtue, which is His power within us.

<u>John 15:1-1 (KJV)</u> 'Abide in Me'

1 I am the true vine, and my Father is the husbandman.

2 Every branch in me that beareth not fruit he taketh away: and every branch that beareth fruit, he purgeth it, that it may bring forth more fruit.

3 Now ye are clean through the word which I have spoken unto you. 4 Abide in me, and I in you. As the branch cannot bear fruit of itself, except it abides in the vine; no more can ye, except ye abide in me.

5 I am the vine, ye are the branches: He that abideth in me, and I in him, the same bringeth forth much fruit: for without me ye can do nothing.

6 If a man abides not in me, he is cast forth as a branch, and is withered; and men gather them, and cast them into the fire, and they are burned.

7 If ye abide in me, and my words abide in you, ye shall ask what ye will, and it shall be done unto you.

8 Herein is my Father glorified, that ye bear much fruit; so shall ye be my disciples.

9 As the Father hath loved me, so have I loved you: continue ye in my love.

10 If ye keep my commandments, ye shall abide in my love; even as I have kept my Father's commandments, and abide in his love.

What stands out is the word "abide"

JESUS says, we must abide in HIM.

When we abide in Him, we are hidden in Him.

When we are hidden in Him, we partake of Him through our labor with truth (knowledge) and the tokens of the spirit for our activity of faith. Through our activity of faith we are joined to Him and serve God in righteousness. Thereby we keep the commandments of God for our joining to Him that is the terms of His covenant.

Proverbs 10:9

"He that walketh uprightly (spiritually minded) walketh surely: but he that perverteth (carnally) his ways shall be known."

Philippians 4:8-9 (KJV)

8. Finally, brethren, whatsoever things are true, whatsoever things are honest, whatsoever things are just, whatsoever things are pure, whatsoever things are lovely, whatsoever things are of good report; <u>if there be any virtue</u>, and if there be any praise, think on these things.

9. <u>Those things, which ye have both learned, and received</u>, and heard, and seen in me, do: and the God of peace shall be with you.

1 Peter 1:13-16 (KJV) 'without true holiness there can be no virtue' *13. Wherefore <u>gird up the loins of your mind</u>* (take captive all thoughts to Christ Jesus; place all thoughts on the scale of truth, which means choose the knowledge of God and discern the 2 kingdoms presented and choose faith; to discern error from truth, reflect on Me*), be sober(*being alert and focused in labor with the knowledge of salvation and hope*), and hope(*hope in Jesus for the promises fulfilled) *to the end for the grace that is to be brought unto you at the revelation of Jesus Chris(*grace reveals Jesus Chris to the humbled heart, by grace we are called and by grace we increase in faith, as we grow grace upon grace*);*

*14. As obedient children, <u>not fashioning yourselves</u> according to <u>the former lusts</u> in your ignorance (*cease laboring with the knowledge of the world – flesh -, to labor with the knowledge of truth, as projection with imagery is replaced by reflection on Christ building the kingdom of God*):*

*15. But as he (*God*) which hath called (*by grace*) you is <u>holy</u> (*darkness has no hold on Him being pure and undefiled, uncorrupted*), so be <u>ye holy</u>(*separate yourself from the world unto God by His knowledge and tokens*) in all manner of conversation(*prayer, prophesy, preaching, our conversation is now Christ Jesus*);*

16. Because it is written, Be ye holy; for I am holy. (Commandment of the Lord: follow Me and separate yourself unto Me)

Refer vs. 15, *be ye holy in all manner of conversation;*

Seek not to speak of your life and all the issues, needs and contradictions ye suffer, but seek ye rather to please God by keeping Him in remembrance, reflect on His knowledge and let your conversation be Him one to another.

People are inclined to give expression to what they feel and experience in their daily lives. The conversation of the unrighteous reflect their issues, pain and suffering

The conversation of the righteous is Christ who is their new habit of faith. Refer vs. 16, "be ye holy as I am holy"

Holiness:

What is true holiness? "To be holy?"

How can we be holy as God is Holy? Yes. It's possible to be holy as God is Holy. But it requires participation in faith, active involvement, as it's an ongoing process of reciprocation through faiths activity, to remain in that state of holiness.

Holiness is not as the world defines it, for this perception is of man's own understanding gained through religious philosophies based on interpretation of scripture that became a set idea of how a holy person should be and act. And what holiness in fact represents. This conclusion was drawn and molded from the moral code.

The world says:

- Online web -

A life of holiness and total devotion to God

A title given to the Pope or other dignitaries

- Biblestudytools.com -

Holiness of character is ascribed to God-

The quality or state of being holy – used for various religious dignitaries

Sanctification – set apart

- Synonyms: blessedness, devoutness, godliness, piety, piousness, sainthood, saintliness, saintship, sanctity

As you can see, it's all words that depict a certain idea, but nowhere can be found the true meaning of obtaining holiness as a definition of what it really means. The carnal mind cannot understand the spiritual things of God from His perspective; error will prevail through misrepresentation and misconceptions. Spiritual things are understood and discerned by the spiritual minded, baptized with the Holy Spirit, laboring with the tokens of faith sanctified by the blood of Jesus Christ, and thus the *hidden mystery* is revealed by *grace* as the Spirit bears witness to Christ in all things of Him.

God provided Jesus Christ for our sanctification, which means our separation from the world unto Him. Let's read John 17:17, where Jesus speaks unto His Father and says the following:

"13. And now I come to thee; and these things (gospel of salvation= truth) I speak to the world, that they might have my joy (glory=virtue=My substance and temperament=completion in Me through faith in Me) fulfilled in themselves.

14. I have given them thy WORD (truth=Jesus Christ=the pattern and record for faith); *and the world hath* hated (light and darkness do not abide in one space, those whom love darkness will persecute those whom are in the light and of the light) *them, because they are __NOT OF THE WORLD__* (sanctified and holy = set apart from the world unto God through their activity of faith, ceasing to labor with the knowledge and wisdom of the world that was the education of our first birth*), even as I am not of the world.*

15. I pray not that thou shouldest take them out of the world, but that thou shouldest keep them from the evil.(God does not remove the contradictions we suffer and endure daily in life, when one are joined to Him in covenant, but the contradictions remain in order for the heart to be tested and thus Satan, the world and the self to be overcome through faiths activity gaining the overcomer reward)

To obtain true holiness, is to be separated from the curse of death and sin that came upon all seed of the 1st Adam, after his fall from God's grace. We are separated from the world unto the Lord when we enter __into__ Christ, thus abiding in Him through our labor with His knowledge (truth) and the spiritual tokens of our activity of faith daily, as we CEASE to labor with the knowledge and wisdom of the world. Thus we partake of Jesus through our new habit of faith, which is to be co-labourers with Him, as we are kept prisoners of Him. Which means, we are joined to Him by the yoke we carry, through which we are transformed to be new creatures in Christ.

Therefore, *we become holy when we cease to labor with those things that's not profitable for faith and which have corrupted the soul*. Corruption begets a defiled conscience that bears witness to the weak will. In Jesus Christ there is no corruption and thus no darkness prevails in Him. He is holy as His Father is holy and thus so also those who separate themselves through the priesthood of Jesus.

Heb 12:14, *"Follow peace with all men, and __holiness__, __without__ which __no__ __man shall see__ __the Lord.__"*

To conclude:

Without holiness there can be no virtue, for being holy means separation of the self from the knowledge of the world through labor with the knowledge of God and His spiritual contact points /tokens for faith, through which the soul is purged cleansed and healed to take on the likeness of Christ Jesus through regeneration, which is His virtue formed within as the First fruits of the Spirit, by which one is known to be of God, as He sees His reflection within. The fruits of the Spirit are the power of God in the soul, unto glory.

In the absence of holiness, there can be no virtue.

If there is no virtue, then there is no obedience to grace and the fruit born is of darkness.

If there is no virtue, there is no divine transformation taking place.

If there is no virtue, the soul is unacceptable to God and not known by Him, for He knows each one that walks in obedience to His will as He called them forth from out of darkness unto His marvelous light.

Without virtue there is no salvation, even if Jesus died for all sin, taking on Him the responsibility of paying the debt for sin.

Rom 8:5-8

"For they that are <u>after the flesh</u> do mind the things of <u>the flesh</u>; but they that are <u>after the Spirit the things of the Spirit</u>"

For to be carnally minded is <u>death</u>; but to be spiritually minded is <u>life</u> <u>and peace.</u>

Because the <u>carnal mind is enmity</u> against God: for it is not subject to the law of God, neither indeed can be.

So then they that are in the flesh cannot please God

2 Peter 1:2, 3, 4, 5, 9

2. Grace and peace be multiplied unto you through the knowledge of God, and of Jesus Christ our Lord,

3. According as his <u>divine power</u> hath given unto us all things that pertain unto life and godliness, through the knowledge of him that hath called us to <u>glory and</u> <u>virtue</u>:

4. whereby are given unto us exceeding great and precious promises: that by these ye might be partakers of the divine nature, having escaped the corruption that is in the world through lust, 5. And beside this, giving all diligence, <u>add to your faith virtue; and to virtue</u> <u>knowledge;</u>

9. but he that lacketh these things is blind, and cannot see afar off, and hath forgotten that he was purged from his old sins,

What goes in, comes out and reflects the condition of the soul.

What we put in our minds determines what comes out in our words and actions: meaning the knowledge we embrace and choose to empower is the knowledge of influence on our minds and thus it is the substance that we increase with, is what we bear fruit by and so, what proceeds forth from our mouths, is the evidence of the kingdom we do embrace and give testimony too. Program your minds with thoughts that are true, noble, right, pure, lovely, admirable, excellent and praiseworthy.

God has set in each soul His characteristics and thus we have the same. But in remembrance of what is said above, we can't use that for our contact with Him, nor for expression of faith but we can aspire to be good and just in our dealings with our fellow brethren by keeping Christ in mind, reflecting on His truth. When we embrace Christ as our contact point for faith, we are rooted in Him and abide in Him and therefore the affections of the heart changes, our appetite changes, from that of the flesh (world) to that of the Spirit. This becomes our new habit of faith and by virtue formed within the soul, there is no effort in being like Him, for peace rules the heart that is not of the world but of the Lord that exceeds the reason and understanding of the carnal mind. Therefore we are governed by the Spirit of righteousness and we express the virtue of Him through our reactions to offenses / contradictions suffered in times of testing of faith.

Love thy neighbor as thou love thyself by the charity that proceeds forth from your lips. Charity reflects Jesus Christ and is the gift offered unto God that equals the gift he gave us, Jesus Christ our Lord.

Do you have problems with impure thoughts and daydreams?

Examine what you are putting into your minds through television, internet, books, conversations, movies, and magazines. Replace harmful input with wholesome material.

Everything we are exposed to is designed to remove faith from Christ and place it in the self, no matter how obsolete it may seem. What we choose to partake of, either takes us on the narrow way or the broadway, the way of life eternal or the way of death eternal. Man received free will and God does not force anyone to be obedient, it's a choice you make on your own and will be judged for your works when the time comes.

The battle for your soul starts in the mind and is won or lost in the mind.

Read the word of God and pray.

Prayer is the communication of the righteous. Study and be approved of by the Lord.

Petition the Lord to show you the way of His truth and be joined to Him in righteousness.

JESUS SAID in JOHN 14:26, *"But the Comforter, which is the Holy Ghost, whom the Father will send in my name, he shall teach you all things, and bring all things to your remembrance, whatsoever I have said unto you."*

It's not enough to hear or read the word of God or even to know it well. We must put it into practice.

When put in practice, we refer to an activity of faith that is sanctified by God and brings life to the soul. Doing righteousness is to labor with His knowledge and the tokens by which we touch Him and are so healed from the scars of our 1st birth, through fruit-bearing unto virtue that is the power of God in the soul that pleases the Father.

How easy is it to hear a sermon and forget what it said?

How easy is it to read the bible and not live what it says and live differently?

Exposure to scripture alone, will not bring forth transformation of the soul, for divine change is by divine power and as said before, an activity of faith under His stewardship by which the power of the Spirit makes faith living.

When a believer is joined to God in covenant, truth is laid within the heart and becomes a living substance not to be forgotten as the Spirit breaks open understanding of the mystery of Christ in truth.

Many believers want the abundance of God's grace and peace, but they are unwilling to put forth the effort to get to know HIM better through study and prayer. To enjoy the privileges God offers us freely, we have "the knowledge of God and hope in JESUS OUR LORD for fulfillment of His promises". The power to grow in faith does not come from within us, but is by the grace of God.

Of our own, we can't be truly godly (good), but God has given us a place where to we can go to find Him and get to know Him and thus be of divine nature through the virtue born within, in order to free us from sin and help us live not by sight but by faith, unto glory of HIM. When we are born again, God by HIS spirit empowers us with HIS own goodness, fruits of the Spirit.

Matthew 22: 36 -39

36 Master, which is the great commandment in the law? 37Jesus said unto him, Thou shalt love the Lord thy God with all thy heart, and with all thy soul, and with all thy mind.

38 This is the first and great commandment.

39 And the second is like unto it, Thou shalt love thy neighbor as thyself.

It's time for those asleep to wake from their slumber and embrace the truth of the Lord upholding His terms for salvation, by which we are saved through grace.

Grace, as the power of God, awakens the heart to want to know God, seek God and walk in equity(agreement) with God as faith is drawn from the heart, being single-and sober-minded.

By grace ye are called and by grace ye are saved.

Grace sustains the obedient unto growth and increase as the fruits of our labor (virtue) beautifies the soul, being a testimony of the Operation of God within the soul.

When the Lord comes a knocking, you will have the choice to accept Him in truth as grace reveals Him to you or resist His grace and thus turn away from the Lord, there is no shortcuts to heaven, the only way is the narrow way that requires participation in faith with His knowledge and tokens for faiths labor under His Stewardship. The Lord resists the proud and accepts the humble.

Resisting grace you resist God and are called a sinner.

The yoke of the Lord is simple and the burden is light, be ye not turned by the fear of man, but know the fear of God, for only a fool perceive the things of His kingdom foolishness, for he as a fool rejects the Hand of the Lord.

John 14: 17 - 21,

"17. Even the <u>Spirit of truth</u>; whom the world <u>cannot receive</u>, because it <u>seeth him not, neither knoweth him</u>: but ye know him; for he dwelleth with you, and shall be in you."

No man can out of his own, see the face of Christ in truth unless it be given by God, for the eyes and ears of man has been closed to not see Christ Jesus, by the system of sin that is the system of false knowledge and the inheritance of our first birth, that beareth fruits of iniquity. Those who are blinded by the false light of darkness see not the true light that will lead them from bondage unto liberty.

The spiritual minded have received the gift of salvation and in turn give back unto the Lord that which is equal to His gift, Jesus Christ our Lord, by the words they speak they glorify His name, thus they are received by Him to be of HIM.

We can only know Him by His knowledge when joined to Him in His covenant of the Spirit, for this is the fruitful womb of our rebirth unto righteousness, holiness, peace and the first fruits of our salvation.

Those of the Spirit are the seed of Abraham whom was found of the Lord to be righteous through faith; they are the lot of the Father whom has called them out of darkness unto His marvelous light, to be a peculiar people, a holy nation, undefiled and pure as they are separated from sinners unto the Lord.

The Spirit dwelleth in those baptized in the Spirit that carry the yoke of Christ unto eternal life in and through Him. As the Father is in them, so they are in Him, being hidden in Christ. By the power of His Spirit the righteous know Him, as He bears witness to the Son.

18 I will not leave you comfortless: I will come to you.

Jesus Christ did send us the comforter to dwell in those who follow Him. He was transcended into heaven but in His place we received the Holy Spirit to bear witness to Him and to effect the divine transformation of the old man to the new man within those pure and holy.

19 Yet a little while, and the world seeth me no more; but ye see me: because I live, ye shall live also.

We see Him by grace and truth, and thus His Spirit is with us to reveal Him to us by grace as we conform to truth (holy knowledge).

20 On that day ye shall know that I am in my Father, and ye in me, and I in you.

Speaks of true unity of the Spirit, the Father in the Son and the Son in the righteous, thus the righteous are in the Son as He is in the Father, so they are in the Father: United in One Spirit.

21 He that hath my commandments, and keepeth them, he it is that loveth me: and he that loveth me shall be loved of my Father, and I will love him, and will manifest myself to him.

God manifests Himself unto the faithful through the gifts of the Spirit and His manifold of graces, by which they are edified and comforted and increase in knowledge, understanding and wisdom that are not earthbound but heaven bound.

He is manifested IN them by the fruits of the Spirit and the presence of His peace within, for their endurance in faith, strengthened by the charity of the brethren.

Hebrews 10:30 (KJV) 'Judge'

"For we know him that hath said, Vengeance belongeth unto me, I will recompense, saith the Lord. And again, The Lord shall judge his people"

Romans 14:10-13 (KJV) 'Judge'

10 But why don't you judge thy brother? or why dost thou set at nought thy brother? for we shall all stand before the judgment seat of Christ.

11 For it is written, As I live, saith the Lord, every knee shall bow to me, and every tongue shall confess to God.

12 So then every one of us shall give account of himself to God. 13 Let us not therefore judge one another any more: but judge this rather, that no man put a stumbling block or an occasion to fall in his brother's way.

The Lord shall judge each man according to his works and no man shall be hid from it. For He is known by those who in humbleness seek Him unto life and all goodness, as Christ Jesus is manifested in them (virtue) and to (manifold graces and gifts of the Spirit) them.

But woe unto them who sought to pervert the ways of the Lord and sought their own council doing works of the flesh, for Christ is not in these works and the fruits thereof is of no substance to the soul for life and increase but unto death and decrease.

So, each man shall be revealed to be of mercy or to be of wrath by the fruit born within which will bear evidence against them or to be a witness for them of their obedience to the will of God

Virtue is the key to Salvation

The only way we can receive it and maintain it is through JESUS CHRIST as our contact point for faith, we must become a HOLY PEOPLE OF GOD following Him in Spirit and Truth, serving Him in righteousness unto His glory.

JESUS CHRIST IS THE WAY, THE TRUTH AND LIFE.

AMEN.

Jesus Walk On Water

Matthew 14:22-33. This story is also told in Mark 6:45-52 and John 6:16-21, however, the account of Peter walking on the water is not included in these references. After feeding the 5000, Jesus sends his disciples ahead of him in a boat to cross the Sea of Galilee. Several hours later in the night, the disciples encounter a storm. Jesus comes to them, walking on the water. This terrifies the disciples who think they are seeing a ghost. Jesus tells them in verse 27, "Take courage! It is I. Don't be afraid."

Peter replies, "Lord, if it's you, tell me to come to you on the water." So Jesus invites Peter to come. Peter gets out of the boat and begins walking on the water toward Jesus. But when Peter takes his eyes off Jesus and sees the wind and waves, he begins to sink. Peter cries out to the Lord and Jesus immediately reaches out his hand and catches Peter. As they climb into the boat together, the storm ceases. Then the disciples worship Jesus, saying, "Truly you are the Son of God." Jesus sends the disciples away so he can get alone on the mountainside and pray. Even in his busy schedule, spending time with God is a priority for Jesus. The disciples, even though they have spent much time with Jesus, don't recognize him in the storm. Sometimes we don't recognize the Lord when he comes to us in the middle of our "storms." Peter doesn't begin to sink until he starts looking around at the wind and the waves. Taking our eyes off Jesus, and focusing on the difficult circumstances will cause us to get under our problems. But when we cry out to Jesus, he catches us by the hand and raises us above the seemingly impossible surroundings. Peter starts out with good intentions, but his faith falters. This does not, however, end up in failure. Peter, even in his fear, cries out to the Lord, the only one who can help him. When Jesus gets in the boat, the storm ceases. When we have Jesus "in our boat" the storms of life will be calmed and we can worship Him. Though we may not walk across water, we will go through difficult, faith-testing circumstances. Are you sinking into despair or are you looking to Jesus and his miraculous power for help? Then the answer is to seek and find

JESUS walk in all his ways Amen

David and GOLIATH

A Philistine giant measuring over nine feet tall and wearing full armor came out each day for forty days, mocking and challenging the Israelites to fight. His name was Goliath. Saul, the King of Israel, and the whole army were terrified of Goliath.

One day David, the youngest son of Jesse, was sent to the battle lines by his father to bring back news of his brothers. David was probably just a young teenager at the time. While there, David heard Goliath shouting his daily defiance and he saw the great fear stirred within the men of Israel. David responded, "Who is this uncircumcised Philistine that he should defy the armies of God?"

So David volunteered to fight Goliath. It took some persuasion, but King Saul finally agreed to let David fight against the giant. Dressed in his simple tunic, carrying his shepherd's staff, sling and a pouch full of stones, David approached Goliath. The giant cursed at him, hurling threats and insults.

David said to the Philistine, "You come against me with sword and spear and javelin, but I come against you in the name of the Lord Almighty, the God of the armies of Israel, whom you have defiled ... today I will give the carcasses of the Philistine army to the birds of the air ... and the whole world will know that there is a God in Israel ... it is not by sword or spear that the Lord saves; for the battle is the Lord's, and he will give all of you into our hands."

As Goliath moved in for the kill, David reached into his bag and slung one of his stones at Goliath's head. Finding a hole in the armor, the stone sank into the giant's forehead and he fell face down on the ground. David then took Goliath's sword, killed him and then cut off his head. When the Philistines saw that their hero was dead, they turned and ran. So the Israelites pursued, chasing and killing them and plundering their camp. Why did they wait forty days to begin the battle? Probably for several reasons. Everyone was afraid of Goliath.

He seemed invincible. Not even King Saul, the tallest man in Israel, had stepped out to fight. Also, the sides of the valley were very steep. Whoever made the first move would have a strong disadvantage and probably suffer great loss. Both sides were waiting for the other to attack first.

- David chose not to wear the King's armor because it felt cumbersome and unfamiliar. David was comfortable with his simple sling, a weapon he was skilled at using. God will use the unique skills he's already placed in your hands, so don't worry about "wearing the King's armor." Just be yourself and use the familiar gifts and talents God has given you. He will work miracles through you.

- David's faith in God caused him to look at the giant from a different perspective. Goliath was merely a mortal man defying an all-powerful God. David looked at the battle from God's point of view. If we look at giant problems and impossible situations from God's perspective, we realize that God will fight for us and with us. When we put things in proper perspective, we see more clearly and we can fight more effectively. When the giant criticized, insulted and threatened, David didn't stop or even waver. Everyone else cowered in fear, but David ran to the battle. He knew that action needed to be taken. David did the right thing in spite of discouraging insults and fearful threats. Only God's opinion mattered to David. Are you facing a giant problem or impossible situation? Stop for a minute and refocus. Can you see the situation more clearly from God's vantage point?

Do you need to take courageous action in the face of insults and fearful circumstances? Do you trust that God will fight for you and with you? Remember, God's opinion is the only one that matters

Woman at the Well

This story shows that their in no one unreachable to come to JESUS so we as faithful servants to the LORD must look to everyone we must become HOLY and abide in JESUS to fulfill this work our hearts must be open to all people. John 4:1-40.Traveling from Jerusalem in the south to Galilee in the north, Jesus and his disciples took the quickest route, through Samaria. Tired and thirsty, Jesus sat by Jacob's Well, while his disciples went to the village of Sychar, about a half mile away, to buy food. It was about noon, the hottest part of the day, and a Samaritan woman came to the well at this inconvenient time, to draw water.

In his encounter with the woman at the well, Jesus broke three Jewish customs: first, he spoke to a woman; second, she was a Samaritan woman, a group the Jews traditionally despised; and third, he asked her to get him a drink of water, which would have made him ceremonially unclean from using her cup or jar. This shocked the woman at the well.

Then Jesus told the woman he could give her "living water" so that she would never thirst again. Jesus used the words living water to refer to eternal life, the gift that would satisfy her soul's desire only available through him. At first, the Samaritan woman didn't fully understand Jesus' meaning.

Although they had never met before, Jesus revealed that he knew she had had five husbands and was now living with a man who was not her husband. Jesus now had her attention! As they talked about their two views on worship, the woman voiced her faith that Messiah was coming. Jesus answered, "I who speak to you am he." (John 4:26,~} As the woman began to grasp the reality of her encounter with Jesus, the disciples returned. They were equally shocked to find him speaking to a woman. Leaving behind her water jar, the woman returned to town, inviting the people to "Come, see a man who told me all that I ever did." (John 4:29,} Meanwhile, Jesus told his disciples the harvest of souls was already sewn by the prophets, writers of the Old Testament, and John the Baptist.

Excited by what the woman told them, the Samaritans came from Sychar and begged Jesus to stay with them.

So Jesus stayed two days, teaching the Samaritan people about the Kingdom of God. When he left, the people told the woman, "... we have heard for ourselves, and we know that this is indeed the Savior of the world." (John 4:42,}• The Samaritans were a mixed race people, who had intermarried with the Assyrians centuries before. They were hated by the Jews because of this cultural mixing, and because they had their own version of the Bible and their own temple on Mount Gerizim.

- The woman at the well came to draw water at the hottest part of the day, instead of the usual morning or evening times, because she was shunned and rejected by the other women of the area for her immorality. Jesus knew her history but still accepted her and ministered to her.

- By reaching out to the Samaritans, Jesus showed that his mission was to the entire earth, not just the Jews. In the book of Acts, after Jesus' ascension into heaven, his apostles carried on his work in Samaria and to the Gentile world.

- Ironically, while the High Priest and Sanhedrin rejected Jesus as the Messiah, the outcast Samaritans recognized him and accepted him for who he truly was: the Savior of the world. Our human tendency is to judge others because of stereotypes, customs or prejudices. Jesus treats people as individuals, accepting them with love and compassion.

Do you dismiss certain people as lost causes, or do you see them as valuable in their own right, worthy of knowing about the gospel? If you call yourself a true Christian you must become and behave as JESUS did people who put themselves first, are not where they think they are, when JESUS judges us we will be judged on all these things our rewards showed not be of this world but in our promise of eternal life our rewards are in HEAVEN Amen.

Jonah and the Whale

GOD tells Jonah to go to Nineveh but he goes and runs the other way are you running from GOD'S plan for you if you are think again this story will tell you why.The story of Jonah and the Whale, one of the oddest accounts in the Bible, opens with God speaking to Jonah, son of Amittai, commanding him to preach repentance to the city of Nineveh.

Jonah found this order unbearable. Not only was Nineveh known for its wickedness, but it was also the capital of the Assyrian empire, one of Israel's fiercest enemies. Jonah, a stubborn fellow, did just the opposite of what he was told. He went down to the seaport of Joppa and booked passage on a ship to Tarshish, heading directly away from Nineveh. The Bible tells us Jonah "ran away from the Lord."

In response, God sent a violent storm, which threatened to break the ship to pieces. The terrified crew cast lots, determining that Jonah was responsible for the storm. Jonah told them to throw him overboard. First they tried rowing to shore, but the waves got even higher. Afraid of God, the sailors finally tossed Jonah into the sea, and the water immediately grew calm. The crew made a sacrifice to God, swearing vows to him.

Instead of drowning, Jonah was swallowed by a great fish, which God provided. In the belly of the whale, Jonah repented and cried out to God in prayer. He praised God, ending with the eerily prophetic statement, "Salvation comes from the Lord." (Jonah 2:9,}Jonah was in the giant fish for three days. God commanded the whale, and it vomited the reluctant prophet onto dry land. This time Jonah obeyed God. He walked through

Nineveh proclaiming that in forty days the city would be destroyed. Surprisingly, the Ninevites believed Jonah's message and repented, wearing sackcloth and covering themselves in ashes. God had compassion on them and did not destroy them.

Again Jonah questioned God, because Jonah was angry that Israel's enemies had been spared. When Jonah stopped outside the city to rest, God provided a vine to shelter him from the hot sun. Jonah was happy with the vine, but the next day God provided a worm that ate the vine, making it wither. Growing faint in the sun, Jonah complained again.

God scolded Jonah for being concerned about a vine, but not about Nineveh, which had 120,000 lost people. The story ends with God expressing concern even about the wicked. God commands everything in his Creation, from the weather to a whale, to carry out his plan. God is in control. Jonah spent the same amount of time—three days—inside the whale as Jesus Christ did in the tomb. Christ also preached salvation to the lost. It's not important whether it was a great fish or a whale that swallowed Jonah. The point of the story is that God can provide a supernatural means of rescue when his people are in trouble. Some scholars believe the Ninevites paid attention to Jonah because of his bizarre appearance. They speculate that the whale's stomach acid bleached Jonah's hair, skin, and clothing a ghostly white. Jesus did not consider the book of Jonah to be a fable or myth. While modern skeptics may find it impossible that a man could survive inside a great fish for three days, Jesus compared himself to Jonah, showing that this prophet existed and that the story was historically accurate. Jonah thought he knew better than God. But in the end he learned a valuable lesson about the Lord's mercy and forgiveness, which extends beyond Jonah and Israel to all people who repent and believe. Is there some area of your life in which you are defying God, and rationalizing it? Remember that God wants you to be open and honest with him. It's always wise to obey the One who loves you most. Brothers and Sisters if GOD has called you stop running away because just as Jonah did in the end what he was told to. You also will if GOD has to bring you to your knees HE will, so listen now, don't be a Jonah amen.

Parable of Prodigal Son

The Parable of the Prodigal Son is found in Luke chapter 15, verses 11-32. The main character in the parable, the forgiving father, whose character remains constant throughout the story, is a picture of God. In telling the story, Jesus identifies Himself with God in His loving attitude to the lost. The younger son symbolizes the lost (the tax collectors and sinners of that day, Luke 15:1), and the elder brother represents the self-righteous (the Pharisees and teachers of the law of that day, Luke 15:2). The major theme of this parable seems not to be so much the conversion of the sinner, as in the previous two parables of Luke 15, but rather the restoration of a believer into fellowship with the Father. In the first two parables, the owner went out to look for what was lost (Luke 15:110), whereas in this story the father waits and watches eagerly for his son's return. We see a progression through the three parables from the relationship of one in a hundred (Luke 15:1-7), to one in ten (Luke 15:8-10), to one in one (Luke 15:11-32), demonstrating God's love for each individual and His personal attentiveness towards all humanity. We see in this story the graciousness of the father overshadowing the sinfulness of the son, as it is the memory of the father's goodness that brings the prodigal son to repentance (Romans 2:4).

We will begin unfolding the meaning of this parable at verse 12, in which the younger son asks his father for his share of his estate, which would have been half of what his older brother would receive; in other words, 1/3 for the younger, 2/3 for the older (Deuteronomy 21:17). Though it was perfectly within his rights to ask, it was not a loving thing to do, as it implied that he wished his father dead. Instead of rebuking his son, the father patiently grants him his request. This is a picture of God letting a sinner go his own way (Deuteronomy 30:19). We all possess this foolish ambition to be independent, which is at the root of the sinner persisting in his sin (Genesis 3:6;Romans 1:28). A sinful state is a departure and distance from God (Romans 1:21). A sinful state is also a state of constant discontent.Luke 12:15 says, "Watch out! Be on your guard against all kinds of greed; a man's life does not consist in the abundance of his possessions." This son learned the hard way that covetousness leads to a life of dissatisfaction and disappointment. He also learned that the most valuable things in life are the things you cannot buy or replace.

In verse 13 we read that he travels to a distant country. It is evident from his previous actions that he had already made that journey in his heart, and the physical departure was a display of his willful disobedience to all the goodness his father had offered (Proverbs 27:19;Matthew 6:21;12:34). In the process, he squanders all his father had worked so hard for on selfish, shallow fulfillment, losing everything. His financial disaster is followed by a natural disaster in the form of a famine, which he failed to plan for (Genesis 41:33-36). At this point he sells himself into physical slavery to a Gentile and finds himself feeding pigs, a detestable job to the Jewish people (Leviticus 11:7;Deuteronomy 14:8;Isaiah 65:4;66:17). Needless to say, he must have been incredibly desperate at that point to willingly enter into such a loathsome position. And what an irony that his choices led him to a position in which he had no choice but to work, and for a stranger at that, doing the very things he refused to do for his father. To top it off, he apparently was paid so little that he longed to eat the pig's food. Just when he must have thought life could not get any worse, he couldn't even find mercy among the people. Apparently, once his wealth was gone, so were his friends. The text clearly says, "No one gave him anything" (vs. 16). Even these unclean animals seemed to be better off than he was at this point. This is a picture of the state of the lost sinner or a rebellious Christian who has returned to a life of slavery to sin (2 Peter 2:19-21). It is a picture of what sin really does in a person's life when he rejects the Father's will (Hebrews 12:1;Acts 8:23). "Sin always promises more than it gives, takes you further than you wanted to go, and leaves you worse off than you were before." Sin promises freedom but brings slavery (John 6:23).

The son begins to reflect on his condition and realizes that even his father's servants had it better than he. His painful circumstances help him to see his father in a new light and bring him hope (Psalm 147:11;Isaiah 40:30-31;Romans 8:24-25;1 Timothy 4:10). This is reflective of the sinner when he/she discovers the destitute condition of his life because of sin. It is a realization that, apart from God, there is no hope (Ephesians 2:12;2 Timothy 2:25-26). This is when a repentant sinner "comes to his senses" and longs to return to the state of fellowship with God which was lost when Adam sinned (Genesis 3:8). The son devises a plan of action. Though at a quick glance it may seem that he may not be truly repentant, but rather motivated by his hunger, a more thorough study of the text gives new insights. He is willing to give up his rights as his father's son and take on the position of his servant. We can only speculate on this point, but he may even have been willing to repay what he had lost (Luke 19:8;Leviticus 6:4-5). Regardless of the motivation, it demonstrates a true humility and true repentance, not based on what he said but on what he was willing to do and eventually acted upon (Acts 26:20). He realizes he has no right to claim a blessing upon return to his father's household, nor does he have anything to offer, except a life of service, in repentance of his previous actions. With that, he is prepared to fall at his father's feet and hope for forgiveness and mercy. This is exactly what conversion is all about: ending a life of slavery to sin through confession to the Father and faith in Jesus Christ and becoming a slave to righteousness, offering one's body as a living sacrifice (1 John 1:9;Romans 6:6-18;12:1).

Jesus portrays the father as waiting for his son, perhaps daily searching the distant road, hoping for his appearance. The father noticed him while he was still a long way off. The father's compassion assumes some knowledge of the son's pitiful state, possibly from reports sent home. During that time it was not the custom of men to run, yet the father runs to greet his son (vs.20).

Why would he break convention for this wayward child who had sinned against him? The obvious answer is because he loved him and was eager to show him that love and restore the relationship. When the father reaches his son, not only does he throw his arms around him, but he also greets him with a kiss of love (1 Peter 5:14). He is so filled with joy at his son's return that he doesn't even let him finish his confession. Nor does he question or lecture him; instead, he unconditionally forgives him and accepts him back into fellowship. The father running to his son, greeting him with a kiss and ordering the celebration is a picture of how our Heavenly Father feels towards sinners who repent.

God greatly loves us, patiently waits for us to repent so he can show us His great mercy, because he does not want any to perish nor escape as though by the fire (Ephesians 2:1-10;2 Peter 3:9;1 Corinthians 3:15).

This prodigal son was satisfied to return home as a slave, but to his surprise and delight is restored back into the full privilege of being his father's son. He had been transformed from a state of destitution to complete restoration. That is what God's grace does for a penitent sinner (Psalm 40:2;103:4). Not only are we forgiven, but we receive a spirit of sonship as His children, heirs of God and co-heirs with Christ, of His incomparable riches (Romans 8:16-17;Ephesians 1:18-19). The father then orders the servants to bring the best robe, no doubt one of his own (a sign of dignity and honor, proof of the prodigal's acceptance back into the family), a ring for the son's hand (a sign of authority and son ship) and sandals for his feet (a sign of not being a servant, as servants did not wear shoes—or, for that matter, rings or expensive clothing, vs.22). All these things represent what we receive in Christ upon salvation: the robe of the Redeemer's righteousness (Isaiah 61:10), the privilege of partaking of the Spirit of adoption (Ephesians 1:5), and feet fitted with the readiness that comes from the gospel of peace, prepared to walk in the ways of holiness (Ephesians 6:15). A fattened calf is prepared, and a party is held (notice that blood was shed = atonement for sin, Hebrews 9:22). Fated calves in those times were saved for special occasions such as the Day of Atonement (Leviticus 23:26-32). This was not just any party; it was a rare and complete celebration. Had the boy been dealt with according to the Law, there would have been a funeral, not a celebration. "The Lord does not treat us as our sins deserve or repay us according to our iniquities. For as high as the heavens are above the earth, so great is his love for those who fear him; as far as the east is from the west, so far has he removed our transgressions from us. As a father has compassion on his children, so the Lord has compassion on those who fear him." (Psalm 103:10-13). Instead of condemnation, there is rejoicing for a son who had been dead but now is alive, who once was lost but now is found (Romans 8:1;John 5:24). Note the parallel between "dead" and "alive" and "lost" and "found"—terms that also apply to one's state before and after conversion to Christ (Ephesians 2:15). This is a picture of what occurs in heaven over one repentant sinner (Luke 15: 7,10).

Now to the final and tragic character in the Parable of the Prodigal Son, the oldest son, who, once again, illustrates the Pharisees and the scribes. Outwardly they lived blameless lives, but inwardly their attitudes were abominable (Matthew 23:25-28). This was true of the older son who worked hard, obeyed his father, and brought no disgrace to his family or townspeople. It is obvious by his words and actions, upon his brother's return, that he is not showing love for his father or brother. One of the duties of the eldest son would have included reconciliation between the father and his son. He would have been the host at the feast to celebrate his brother's return. Yet he remains in the field instead of in the house where he should have been. This act alone would have brought public disgrace upon the father. Still, the father, with great patience, goes to his angry and hurting son. He does not rebuke him as his actions and disrespectful address of his father warrant (vs.29, "Look," he says, instead of addressing him as "father" or "my lord"), nor does his compassion cease as he listens to his complaints and criticisms. The boy appeals to his father's righteousness by proudly proclaiming his own self-righteousness in comparison to his brother's sinfulness (Matthew 7:3-5).

By saying, "This son of yours," the older brother avoids acknowledging that the prodigal is his own brother (vs. 30). Just like the Pharisees, the older brother was defining sin by outward actions, not inward attitudes (Luke 18:9-14). In essence, the older brother is saying that he was the one worthy of the celebration, and his father had been ungrateful for all his work. Now the one who had squandered his wealth was getting what he, the older son, deserved. The father tenderly addresses his oldest as "my son" (vs. 31) and corrects the error in his thinking by referring to the prodigal son as "this brother of yours" (vs. 32). The father's response, "We had to celebrate," suggests that the elder brother should have joined in the celebration, as there seems to be a sense of urgency in not postponing the celebration of the brother's return.

The older brother's focus was on himself, and as a result there is no joy in his brother's arrival home. He is so consumed with issues of justice and equity that he fails to see the value of his brother's repentance and return. He fails to realize that "anyone who claims to be in the light but hates his brother is still in the darkness. Whoever loves his brother lives in the light, and there is nothing in him to make him stumble. But whoever hates his brother is in the darkness; he does not know where he is going, because the darkness has blinded him" (1 John 2:9-11). The older brother allows anger to take root in his heart to the point that he is unable to show compassion towards his brother, and, for that matter he is unable to forgive the perceived sin of his father against him (Genesis 4:5-8). He prefers to nurse his anger rather than enjoy fellowship with his father, brother and the community. He chooses suffering and isolation over restoration and reconciliation (Matthew 5:24,6:14-15). He sees his brother's return as a threat to his own inheritance. After all, why should he have to share his portion with a brother who has squandered his? And why hadn't his father rejoiced in his presence through his faithful years of service?

The wise father seeks to bring restoration by pointing out that all he has is and has always been available for the asking to his obedient son, as it was his portion of the inheritance since the time of the allotment. The older son never utilized the blessings at his disposal (Galatians 5:22;2 Peter 1:5-8). This is similar to the Pharisees with their religion of good works. They hoped to earn blessings from God and in their obedience merit eternal life (Romans 9:31-33;10:3). They failed to understand the grace of God and failed to comprehend the meaning of forgiveness. It was, therefore, not what they did that became a stumbling block to their growth but rather what they did not do which alienated them from God (Matthew 23:23-24, Romans 10:4). They were irate when Jesus was receiving and forgiving "unholy" people, failing to see their own need for a Savior. We do not know how this story ended for the oldest son, but we do know that the Pharisees continued to oppose Jesus and separate themselves from His followers. Despite the father's pleading for them to "come in," they refused and were the ones who instigated the arrest and crucifixion of Jesus Christ (Matthew 26:59). A tragic ending to a story filled with such hope, mercy, joy, and forgiveness.

The picture of the father receiving the son back into the relationship is a picture of how we should respond to repentant sinners as well (1 John 4:20-21;Luke 17:3;Galatians 6:1;James 5:19-20). "All have sinned and fall short of the glory of God " (Romans 3:23). We are included in that "all," and we must remember that "all our righteous acts are like filthy rags" apart from Christ (Isaiah 64:6;John 15:1-6). It's Only by God's grace that we are saved, not by works that we may boast of (Ephesians 2:9;Romans

9:16;Psalm 51:5). That is the core message of the Parable of the Prodigal Son.

Mysteries of the LORD Revealed

Today's mystery of the Lord revealed is of the book of Isaiah about the prophet Isaiah.... The grafted branch of the gentiles, the man raised by Elisha's bones, the first prophet to preach the coming of the Messiah Jesus.

As the last mystery revealed takes us to King Solomon, we see Solomon fall into evil by losing faith and praising false idols thus receiving the mark of the beast 666 and turning away from the Lord and His commands.

The lineage of King David to the Messiah is thus broken by the falling away of King David's son Solomon and must be repaired.

Romans 11:

11 I say then, have they stumbled that they should fall? Certainly not! But through their fall, to provoke them to jealousy, salvation has come to the Gentiles. 12 Now if their fall is riches for the world, and their failure riches for the Gentiles, how much more their fullness! 13 For I speak to you Gentiles; inasmuch as I am an apostle to the Gentiles, I magnify my ministry, 14 if by any means I may provoke jealousy those who are my flesh and save some of them. 15 For if their being cast away is the reconciliation of the world, what will their acceptance be but life from the dead? 16 For if the first fruit is holy, the lump is also holy; and if the root is holy, so are the branches. 17 And if some of the branches were broken off, and you, being a wild olive tree, were grafted in among them, and with them became a partaker of the root and fatness of the olive tree, 18 do not boast against the branches. But if you do boast, remember that you do not

support the root, but the root supports you. 19 You will say then, "Branches were broken off that I might be grafted in." 20 Well said. Because of unbelief they were broken off, and you stand by faith. Do not be haughty, but fearful. 21 For if God did not spare the natural branches, He may not spare you either. 22 Therefore consider the goodness and severity of God: on those who fell, severity; but toward you, goodness, if you continue in His goodness. Otherwise you also will be cut off. 23 And they also, if they do not continue in unbelief, will be grafted in, for God is able to graft them in again. 24 For if you were cut out of the olive tree which is wild by nature, and were grafted contrary to nature into a cultivated olive tree, how much more will these, who are natural branches, be grafted into their own olive tree? 25 For I do not desire, brethren, that you should be ignorant of this mystery, lest you should be wise in your own opinion, that blindness in part has happened to Israel until the fullness of the Gentiles has come in. 26 And so all Israel will be saved, as it is written: "The Deliverer will come out of Zion,

And He will turn away ungodliness from Jacob; 27 For this is My covenant with them, When I take away their sins." 28 Concerning the gospel they are enemies for your sake, but concerning the election they are beloved for the sake of the fathers. 29 For the gifts and the calling of God are irrevocable. 30 For as you were once disobedient to God, yet have now obtained mercy through their disobedience, 31 even so these also have now been disobedient, that through the mercy shown you they also may obtain mercy. 32 For God has committed them all to disobedience, that He might have mercy on all.

Romans 9:

25 As He says also in Hosea:"I will call them My people, who were not My people, And her beloved, who was not beloved."26 "And it shall come to pass in the place where it was said to them, You are not My people, There they shall be called sons of the living God."27 Isaiah also cries out concerning Israel:"Though

the number of the children of Israel be as the sand of the sea, The remnant will be saved.28 For He will finish the work and cut it short in righteousness, Because the Lord will make a short work upon the earth."29 And as Isaiah said before: "Unless the Lord of Sabbath had left us a seed, We would have become like Sodom, And we would have been made like Gomorrah Romans 15:9 and that the Gentiles might glorify God for His mercy, as it is written:"For this reason I will confess to You among the Gentiles, And sing to Your name."10 And again he says: "Rejoice, O Gentiles, with His people!" 11 And again:"Praise the Lord, all you Gentiles! Laud Him, all you people!" 12 And again, Isaiah says: "There shall be a root of Jesse; And He who shall rise to reign over the Gentiles,

In Him the Gentiles shall hope."

Isaiah 10:

And it shall come to pass on that day That the remnant of Israel, And such as have escaped from the house of Jacob, Will never again depend on him who defeated them, But will depend on the Lord, the Holy One of Israel, in truth.

21 The remnant will return, the remnant of Jacob, To the Mighty God.

22 For though your people, O Israel, be as the sand of the sea, A remnant of the will return; The destruction decree shall overflow with righteousness.

23 For the Lord God of hosts Will make a determined end In the midst of all the land.

Isaiah 11

1 There shall come forth a Rod from the stem of Jesse, And a Branch shall grow out of his roots ... .12 He will set up a banner for the nations, And will assemble the outcasts of Israel, And

gather together the dispersed of Judah From the four corners of the earth.

Isaiah in its very meaning translates "Yahweh is Salvation " thus there is no mistake that the book of Yahweh's Salvation comes right after the book of King Solomon which we now know was the turning away of God's people to false idols and lost faith.

Just as Jesus said "I am the resurrection and the Life; he who believes in me will live even if he dies"(John 11:25). Jesus' promise has stood from the very first prophet to preach the coming of Jesus...Isaiah.

Isaiah 7

13 And he said, Hear ye now, O house of David; Is it a small thing for you to weary men, but will ye weary my God also?14 Therefore the Lord himself shall give you a sign; Behold, a virgin shall conceive, and bear a son, and shall call his name Immanuel. 15 Butter and honey shall he eat, that he may know to refuse the evil, and choose the good.

As we know, Isaiah reigned during the days of King Uzzi and preached as much as 64 years, thus dying sometime in the middle of the 7th century.

Elisha died in the 8th century, thus showing that the bones of Elisha could have been in the tomb for as much as a century. Since the timeline of centuries went from highest to smallest Before Christ, this clarifies any doubt.

Elisha was the last house of David, so Elisha's bones carried the second portion rights to raise Isaiah back from the dead to be grafted into God's lineage. Romans 11:

17 And if some of the branches were broken off, and you, being a wild olive tree, were grafted in among them, and with them became a partaker of the root and fatness of the olive tree, 18 do

not boast against the branches. But if you do boast, remember that you do not support the root, but the root supports you.19 You will say then, "Branches were broken off that I might be grafted in."

The bible does not show any more of the living Isaiah and Elijah until the returning of Christ Jesus. Revelations 117 And when they shall have finished their testimony, the beast that ascendant out of the bottomless pit shall make war against them, and shall overcome them, and kill them.8 And their dead bodies shall lie in the street of the great city, which spiritually is called Sodom and Egypt, where also our Lord was crucified.9 And they of the people and kindred and tongues and nations shall see their dead bodies three days and an half, and shall not suffer their dead bodies to be put in graves.10 And they that dwell upon the earth shall rejoice over them, and make merry, and shall send gifts one to another; because these two prophets tormented them that dwelt on the earth.11 And after three days and an half the spirit of life from God entered into them, and they stood upon their feet; and great fear fell upon them which saw them.

The mystery revealed here is that the bible in its entirety speaks of the Lord God (Elijah which represents God's Word) and The Salvation of God (Isaiah which is what the Word of God is all about.).

John 3

For God so loved the world, that he gave his only begotten Son, that whosoever believeth in him should not perish, but have everlasting life.17 For God sent not his Son into the world to condemn the world; but that the world through him might be saved.18 He that believeth on him is not condemned: but he that believeth not is condemned already, because he hath not believed in the name of the only begotten Son of God.

2 timothy 3:

15 And that from a child thou hast known the holy scriptures, which are able to make thee wise unto salvation through faith which is in Christ Jesus.16 All scripture is given by inspiration of God, and is profitable for doctrine, for reproof, for correction, for instruction in righteousness:

REAL WISDOM WILL ALWAYS LEAD TO SALVATION, OR IT IS NOT REAL WISDOM. MYSTERIES REVEALED BY THE HOLY SPIRIT OF GOD WILL ALWAYS LEAD TO JESUS OUR SALVATION.

Amen.

Mysteries of the LORD Revealed

There is something that bothered me when I first read it as a man.

2 Kings 2:9 King James Version

9 And it came to pass, when they were gone over, that Elijah said unto Elisha, Ask what I shall do for thee, before I be taken away from thee. And Elisha said, I pray thee, let a double portion of thy spirit be upon me.

My question as a man was why did Elisha ask for a double portion of Spirit. The reason I asked this was let's look at scripture

1 Kings 17

21 And he stretched himself upon the child three times, and cried unto the Lord, and said, O Lord my God, I pray thee, let this child's soul come into him again.

22 And the Lord heard the voice of Elijah; and the soul of the child came into him again, and he revived.

23 And Elijah took the child, and brought him down out of the chamber into the house, and delivered him unto his mother: and Elijah said, See, thy son liveth.

24 And the woman said to Elijah, Now by this I know that thou art a man of God, and that the word of the Lord in thy mouth is truth.

You see here ELIJAH raised a boy from the dead and many more things he did so i thought surly ELISHA only need the SPIRIT of ELIJAH fall on him. WHY a double portion. Well of course the answer in the secrets of the word lets find the answer lets go to the word

2 Kings 13:20-21 King James Version

20 And Elisha died, and they buried him. And the bands of the Moabites invaded the land at the coming of the year.

21 And it came to pass, as they were burying a man, that, behold, they spied a band of men; and they cast the man into the sepulcher of Elisha: and when the man was let down, and touched the bones of Elisha, he revived, and stood up on his feet.

You see right here is the answer GOD plan was for when ELISHA died this man was going to touch his bones and live. Who is this man do i know yes but for now I cannot say. Now lets go read more Scripture

Romans 8:11-14 King James Version

11 But if the Spirit of him that raised up Jesus from the dead dwells in you, he that raised up Christ from the dead shall also quicken your mortal bodies by his Spirit that dwelleth in you.

12 Therefore, brethren, we are debtors, not to the flesh, to live after the flesh.

13 For if ye live after the flesh, ye shall die: but if ye through the Spirit do mortify the deeds of the body, ye shall live.

14 For as many as are led by the Spirit of God, they are the sons of God.

The double portion was the Spirit that dwelled in ELISHA and the other portion was to raise this man. There is a lot more to

Why all this happened but for now I can't share more but the HOLY SPIRIT can show each and every one of ye. I am but a servant of GOD and the HOLY SPIRIT is my teacher.

John 15:26

26 But when the Comforter is come, whom I will send unto you from the Father, even the Spirit of truth, which proceedeth from the Father, he shall testify of me:

Be blessed brothers and sisters are ye listening Church Amen

Mysteries of the LORD Revealed

Today this is all about King Solomon.

When i was reading about Solomon something bothered me greatly how Solomon turned his back on GOD. Let's look at the word

29 And God gave Solomon wisdom and understanding exceeding much, and largeness of heart, even as the sand that is on the sea shore.

30 And Solomon's wisdom excelled the wisdom of all the children of the east country, and all the wisdom of Egypt.

31 For he was wiser than all men; than Ethan the Ezrahite, and Heman, and Charcoal, and Darda, the sons of Mahol: and his fame was in all nations roundabout.

32 And he spoke three thousand proverbs: and his songs were a thousand and five.

God clearly gave Solomon wisdom it excelled all the wisdom of Egypt so how could a man given this wisdom turn his back on GOD Almighty clearly he did let's look at the word 34 And there came of all people to hear the wisdom of Solomon, from all kings of the earth, which had heard of his wisdom.

1 Kings 11

11 But king Solomon loved many strange women, together with the daughter of Pharaoh, women of the Moabites, Ammonites, Edomites, Zidonians, and Hittites:

2 Of the nations concerning which the Lord said unto the children of Israel, Ye shall not go in to them, neither shall they come in unto you: for surely they will turn away your heart after their gods: Solomon clave unto these in love.

3 And he had seven hundred wives, princesses, and three hundred concubines: and his wives turned away his heart.

4 For it came to pass, when Solomon was old, that his wives turned away his heart after other gods: and his heart was not perfect with the Lord his God, as was the heart of David his father.

5 Solomon went after Ashtoreth the goddess of the Zidonians, and after Milcom the abomination of the Ammonites.

6 And Solomon did evil in the sight of the Lord, and went not fully after the Lord, as did David his father.

7 Then did Solomon build a high place for Chemosh, the abomination of Moab, in the hill that is before Jerusalem, and for Molech, the abomination of the children of Ammon.

8 And likewise did he for all his strange wives, which burnt incense and sacrificed unto their gods.

9 And the Lord was angry with Solomon, because his heart was turned from the Lord God of Israel, which had appeared unto him twice,

God appeared to Solomon twice gave him wisdom yet he turned his back on GOD clearly this shows GOD could not give him HIS wisdom or he would be equal to GOD he gave him man's wisdom and this shows man's wisdom is no good so what really happened to Solomon let's look at the scripture

1 Kings 10

14 Now the weight of gold that came to Solomon in one year was six hundred threescore and six talents of gold,

You see right here Solomon received the mark of Satan look carefully 600=6 3 score a score is twenty =60 =6 and 6 talents =6 the mark 666. How do we know this lets go to Revelation 138 Here is wisdom. Let him that hath understanding count the number of the beast: for it is the number of a man; and his number is Six hundred threescore and six.

See right here is the same mark that fell on Solomon from this time Solomon received it HE turned his back on GOD. Let's look at more scripture

Matthew 6

28 And why are you anxious about clothing? Consider the lilies of the field, how they grow: they neither toil nor spin, 29 yet I tell you, even Solomon in all his glory was not arrayed like one of these.

30 But if God so clothes the grass of the field, which today is alive and tomorrow is thrown into the oven, will he not much more clothe you, O you of little faith?

Luke 12

27 "Consider the lilies, how they grow: they neither toil nor spin; but I tell you, not even Solomon in all his glory clothed himself like one of these

See with all the wealth and everything Solomon had even the flowers which would wither and die are greater than him because he turned his back on GOD. Seal of Solomon

Amos 5:26

"But ye have borne the tabernacle of your Moloch and Chiun your images, the star of your god, which ye made to yourselves."

Acts 7:43

"Yea, ye took up the tabernacle of Moloch, and the star of your god Remphan, figures which ye made to worship them:"

JESUS

Ephesians 1:12-13

"That we should be to the praise of his glory, who first trusted in Christ...in whom also after that ye believed, ye were sealed with that holy Spirit of promise,

Which is the earnestness of our inheritance until the redemption of the purchased possession, unto the praise of his glory."

I Kings 1:46

"And also Solomon sitteth on the throne of the kingdom."

I Chronicles 29:23

"sat on throne of Lord"

JESUS

Luke 1:31-33

"And, behold, thou shalt conceive in thy womb, and bring forth a son, and shall call his name JESUS. He shall be great, and shall be called the Son of the Highest: and the Lord God shall give unto him the throne of his father David: And he shall reign over the house of Jacob forever; and of his kingdom there shall be no end."

Solomon

Matthew 6:29

"And yet I say unto you, That even Solomon in all his glory was not arrayed like one of these."

JESUS

John 1:14

"And the Word was made flesh, and dwelt among us, (and we beheld his glory, the glory as of the only begotten of the Father,) full of grace and truth."

Matthew 25:31

"When the Son of man shall come in his glory, and all the holy angels with him, then shall he sit upon the throne of his glory:"

Solomon

I Kings 1:33,35,45

"So Zadok the priest, and Nathan the prophet, and Benaiah the son of Jehoiada, and the Cherethites, and the Pelethites, went down, and caused Solomon to ride upon king David's mule, and brought him to Gihon. And Zadok the priest took an horn of oil out of the tabernacle, and anointed Solomon.

JESUS

Matthew 3:13-17

"And Jesus, when he was baptized, went up straight-way out of the water: and, lo, the heavens were opened unto him, and he saw the Spirit of God descending like a dove, and lighting upon him:"

Acts 10:38

"How God anointed Jesus of Nazareth with the Holy Ghost and with power:" Solomon

II Chronicles 9:29 "Solomon, first and last"

JESUS

Revelation 1:11

"I was in the Spirit on the Lord's day, and heard behind me a great voice, as of a trumpet, Saying, I am Alpha and Omega"

See the Jews thought Solomon might be the messiah but here is the Appearance of Solomon

Psalm 45 "Thou art fairer than the children of men"

Song of Solomon 5:10-16

"his locks are bushy, and black as a raven" black = darkness.

JESUS

Revelation 1:13-16

"His head and his hairs were white like wool, as white as snow

White = light

These scriptures show the secrets of the word Amen

Mysteries of the LORD Revealed

JESUS turns water into wine and the hidden secrets in this message Let's look at them.

JESUS WAS ON A MISSION TO SAVE THE WORLD, the greatest mission into the history of mankind yet he took time to attend a wedding WHY? Was it to turn water into wine to impress the quest no I should think not. HE was there to save them and for those with wisdom to truly show what HE wanted them to see. Let's look at the scripture JOHN 2 :1-6

The Wedding Feast at Cana

John 2:1-11

1 And the third day there was a marriage in Cana of Galilee; and the mother of Jesus was there:

2 And both Jesus was called, and his disciples, to the marriage.3 And when they wanted wine, the mother of Jesus saith unto him, They have no wine.

4 Jesus saith unto her, Woman, what have I to do with thee? my hour has not yet come.

5 His mother saith unto the servants, Whatsoever he saith unto you, do it.

6 And there were set there six waterpots of stone, after the manner of the purifying of the Jews, containing two or three firkins apiece.

Let's look first at verse 6

JOHN. establishes the setting for Jesus to act. He tells the audience about the presence of six water jars there in the scene (John 2:6). The phrase "for the purification rituals of the Jews" explains why the jars are there. He focuses our attention on the jars long enough to point out considerable detail six count them 6 jars made of stone not clay the most important part of this is they were the kind the JEWS used for ceremonial washing. These jars were all about religious activity. This was the law in those times cleansing by water. So when JESUS turns this water into wine what is the real secret of what HE was showing us. See the water that was to cleanses but JESUS was turning it into HIS blood to show us it was only true HIM after HIS death on the cross that the water that was for cleansing was now HIS blood. Why else would HE say this in verse 4

Jesus saith unto her, Woman, what have I to do with thee? my hour has not yet come.

See this was the start of HIS ministry HE knew HE would have to show signs and wonders for them to believe let's look at this

JOHN 4

46 So Jesus came again into Cana of Galilee, where he made the water wine. And there was a certain nobleman, whose son was sick at Capernaum.

47 When he heard that Jesus had come out of Judaea into Galilee, he went unto him, and besought him that he would come down, and heal his son: for he was at the point of death.

48 Then said Jesus unto him, Except ye see signs and wonders, ye will not believe.

See this man was probably at that wedding and saw what JESUS did when HIS son was dying he came to JESUS.

The six pots represent the days GOD created the world. The water which under the law was for sin all now is now true JESUS only. John 14 6Jesus said to him, "I am the way, and the truth, and the life; no one comes to the Father but through Me.

Mark 7:1-4King James Version (KJV 7 Then came together unto him the Pharisees, and certain of the scribes, which came from Jerusalem.

2 And when they saw some of his disciples eat bread with defiled, that is to say, with unwashen, hands, they found fault.

3 For the Pharisees, and all the Jews, except they wash their hands oft, eat not, holding the tradition of the elders.

4 And when they come from the market, except they wash, they eat not. And many other things there be, which they have received to hold, as the washing of cups, and pots, brasen vessels, and of tables. But by JESUS showing us what was going to happen on the cross here HE CLEARLY shows it's only true HIM we can be saved Amen

Mysteries of the LORD Revealed

This is one verse from the Book of TITUS

The GOSPEL is the living word with many hidden secrets only the HOLY SPIRIT can teach not no man or woman. This book is one most people just skip by TITUS.

Titus 3 verse 5

Titus 3:5 King James Version

6 Not by works of righteousness which we have done, but according to his mercy he saved us, by the washing of regeneration, and renewing of the Holy Ghost;

Now let's look at the message in this scripture through the HOLY SPIRIT. Two very important words here the first one righteousness means smile emoticon goodness, virtue, virtuousness, uprightness, decency, integrity, worthiness, rectitude, probity, morality, ethicalness, high-mindedness, justice, honesty, honor, honourableness, innocence, blamelessness, guiltlessness, irreproachability, sinlessness, saintliness, purity, nobility, noble mindedness, piety, piousness

"The successful are always tempted to regard their success as a reward for righteousness" So let us look at this scripture as regarding to us it says NOT BY WORKS OF RIGHTEOUSNESS all of these things, can we be saved.

The Bible describes the righteous person as just or right, holding to God and trusting in Him (Psalm 33:18–22).

18 Behold, the eye of the Lord is upon them that fear him, upon them that hope in his mercy;

19 To deliver their soul from death, and to keep them alive in famine.

20 Our soul waiteth for the Lord: he is our help and our shield.21 For our heart shall rejoice in him, because we have trusted in his holy name.

22 Let thy mercy, O Lord, be upon us, according as we hope in thee.

No matter what we do by work, the only way we can be saved is through JESUS CHRIST.

The good news is that true righteousness is possible for mankind, but only through the cleansing of sin by Jesus Christ and the indwelling of the Holy Spirit. We have no ability to achieve righteousness in and of ourselves. But Christians possess the righteousness of Christ, because "God made him who had no sin to be sin for us, so that in him we might become the righteousness of God"

(2 Corinthians 5:21).

Corinthians 5: 21 King James Version

21 For he hath made him to be sin for us, who knew no sin; that we might be made the righteousness of God in him. his is an amazing truth. On the cross, Jesus exchanged our sin for His perfect righteousness so that we can one day stand before God and He will see not our sin, but the holy righteousness of the Lord Jesus.

This means that we are made righteous in the sight of God; that is, that we are accepted as righteous and treated as righteous by God on account of what the Lord Jesus has done.

The second important word in this verse is By the washing of Regeneration. Regeneration means born again. How are we born again only true JESUS CHRIST. Regeneration is part of the "salvation package,"

Another word for regeneration is rebirth, from which we get the phrase "born again." To be born again is opposed to, and distinguished from, our first birth, when we were conceived in sin. The new birth is a spiritual, holy, and heavenly birth signified by a being made alive in a spiritual sense. Our first birth, on the other hand, was one of spiritual death because of inherited sin. Man in his natural state is "dead in trespasses and sins" until we are "made alive" (regenerated) by Christ when we place our faith in Him

(Ephesians 2:1-3)

Ephesians 2:1-3 New King James Version By Grace Through Faith

2 And you He made alive, who were dead in trespasses and sins, 2 in which you once walked according to the course of this world, according to the prince of the power of the air, the spirit who now works in the sons of disobedience, 3 among whom also we all once conducted ourselves in the lusts of our flesh, fulfilling the desires of the flesh and of the mind, and were by nature children of wrath, just as the others.

The Bible is clear that the only means of regeneration is by faith in the finished work of Christ on the cross. No amount of good works or keeping of the law can regenerate the heart which from birth is "deceitful and wicked above all things" (Jeremiah 17:9).

9 "The heart is more deceitful than all else And is desperately sick; Who can understand it?

Total regeneration of the heart is necessary for salvation. Paul explains this concept perfectly in Galatians 2:20: "I have been crucified with Christ. It is no longer I who live, but Christ who lives in me. And the life I now live in the flesh I live by faith in the Son of God, who loved me and gave himself for me." This is true regeneration. See church no man or women by any works including baptizing you in water can save you no works of yourself you can give all the money you like to help people that won't save you it is only by the baptism into the death of JESUS CHRIST you can be saved it is the water from HIS side that flowed on the cross that cleanness you and the blood that forgave your sin. Wake up Church to the GOSPEL of truth not men or women Amen.

Prophetic Word

For so sayeth the Lord our God: thou shalt not stand divided against me, but those of true faith shall be united in Me as one, I accept none other than My Son Christ, for so I am the Lord and I have given you all that's profitable of faith but hearken ye to Me?

Thou heareth not My words I speak but follow after thou own imaginations and respect not My covenant, for I say unto you, the day shall come that all shall stand before Me and I shall exalt the pure of Mind but the arrogant and the fretful i shall reject as they reject Me now. Thou listeneth not to my faithful servants but blaspheme against those I Have appointed unto righteousness. I have no mercy for the ignorant but the wise shall prosper in My name as I prosper in them. Seek not your own boundaries for faith but know Me by Mine. I am Lord God of all created in heaven and on earth and so I do My will for My will is righteousness. Sanctify yourself before the face of the Lord for the time is at hand for the return of His bride, spotless and white. Seek not unrighteousness but seek Me in Spirit and truth. I am the Alpha and the Omega, the beginning and the End, I am your destiny, I am the beginning and the end, I shall be glorified in those who are a peculiar people unto Me and in none other shall I find My pleasure. Speak to Me words of wisdom for I am your God and no one shall prevail

In Me that seeks Me not. Harken to My words. I am the light of life and the way.

Prophetic Word

Oh wicked and evil people of Mine

Why do they seek signs and wonders as a testimony of the time and My power?

Do you not know that I am God? That I am who I am? That I am the beginning and the End?

That I am the One that created thee in My Bosom to be born into this world to serve Me and to return unto Me?

Do you think that I am to prove Myself to thee?

Seek not the signs of power but rather seek Me in truth as its given unto thee by the instruction of My holy ones through the apostles doctrine, for only then shall thee see My face in Truth and in Spirit and not revelations that confirms Me not, but seek after the revelation by grace that says, This is My Son in whom I am well pleased. Fornicators of this world, see thee not My power in all things?

For thee are blinded by the faith of this world that testifies only of man and his needs, but not of Me Seek Me in righteousness, for I am the Lord by which all things are made to a life as My life is set into those who abide in Me Forsake not My covenant, for the time is at hand that I will return and glorify those whom have in due process walked after the faith of Abraham, for they are the ones who walked in due process of regeneration and renewing of the mind, to take on My image and likeness as I have determined before the foundations was layd Oh thee hard at heart, speak not in silence and murmur not, for the guile of your heart is known to Me

As the Lord is life and light, so are those who abide in Him, for there is no darkness in Him and no lies, as He is the author of truth that testifies of Christ Jesus, the Blood of the Covenant that He came to fulfill in and through Himself, so that all men could be saved.

Prophetic Word

The soul of man craves for the Light of God - it has been led astray by false doctrine & lies, but through Christ life is returned to the soul so that the soul of man can be completed by the things of God, as one they are, united in one mind and perception, lost no more but found, to remain in His care for all eternity. Thus they who hear the Voice of God, return to Him as one in Christ, answering the Voice of God through obedience in faith, yielding their will to the superiority of God's power to answer through charity, building His nation of Holy Ones unto His glory – forever and ever! Amen!

Glory to God – Glory to our Father, our King of kings! Splendor at His side awaits the obedient, opulence the death of those who hear not His Words, for they live on pretense of knowing Him whom they knoweth not.

Praise God – Almighty Tower of Righteousness, sturdy and strong doth we stand in His Light,

Life given to us by God through Christ, Amen!

Praise God – Almighty Father of all – blessings to receive through Christ, our Brother in faith—

reflecting His glory unto the Father, Father of all, Amen, Amen, Amen!

So be it, so says the Lord.

You hear My voice, answereth My voice, so that you can return unto Life and Light through My Son Christ, Saviour of all you

Righteous Ones, Blessed are you My children of Righteousness, servants of Righteousness...I calleth you – Blessed are you!

Praise God o' Righteous People of Mine,

My nation received from the soil of this earth, resurrected through Christ, are you.

Praise God o' Righteous Ones! Believe in Me, believe in My Word, so sayeth the Lord. Amen!

Praise Him that gave you Life, for in Him you are saved - deliverance are thine!

Walk in the path of righteousness. Deliverance is thine! Praise God – Almighty Father of all Righteous Ones! My vessels of glory are you -

called unto service by the Holy Spirit, blessed are you Holy Ones!

Blessed are you -

Praise God – deliverer of all who walk in cadence with Me, so sayeth the Lord!

Praise Him that gave you Light,

Praise Him who delivered you from evil ways. Praise God o' Righteous Ones!

Praise God -

Glory to all those who love Me in Truth through Christ, My only begotten Son glory unto you all! Amen! Amen! Amen!

Deliverance are yours who walk in My shadow of Light. Praise God!

Praise those who see the face of Christ - for by His reality they live daily, standing strong & upright before Me - reflecting Christ perfectly

-

walking in harmony & in rhythm with the Spirit. Call unto Me & I will deliver on My promises.

So sayeth God your Father Praise Him whom loved you first -

Before the foundations of this world were laid I knoweth you – I loved you – I selected you to be My crowning glory!

Praise God o' Righteous Ones -blaspheme not My Word, My Truth, for I know the hearts of many who knoweth Me not.

They who knoweth Me, walk in cadence with Me, they will harvest the rewards for their faith in Christ. Praise God, o' Righteous Ones!

Blame not one another o' unrighteous for the blame lies not by others but in yourself, your hearts are hardened to the Word of God -

Listen you not to My voice? Speaketh you not the Truth? For I know the words of the unrighteous spoken in silence, for that I knoweth your hearts!

Blaspheme you not My Word, My Truth, o' dark ones? Speaketh you not Words of death & evil ways to one another?

Speaketh you not unto death to one another? Mislead not one another, for the rewards of your evil ways are death.

Praise you not your idols of imagery...of magnitude...of lust..of deceit? Walk in the shadows of death unto death, but you..

being called unto My servitude shall inherit eternal life as your reward for obedience in faith, is life eternal – for ever and ever. Praise you not the imaginations of one another o' blasphemers of My Truth in Christ?

Exalt you not yourself above Me? Buildeth you not houses upon the sands of imagery, protecting one another with vain imaginations? Build your houses upon My Rock -

His foundation is eternal and everlasting – for all times to come! Blaspheme not My name, for you provoke Me to anger so sayeth the Lord your God!

I speaketh Words of Wisdom unto those who have ears to hear, I reciprocate in kind unto those who love Me unto death – for dying unto Me is your servitude! Listen to My Words and harken to My Voice, deliverance will be soon unto the obedient. Deliverance of the Righteous, I call My own. Praise

God o' Righteous Ones, forsake not your God – for His ways are

Righteousness,

Praise Him with all your might and power given unto you by Me. Praise Him who loved you first!

Amen! Amen! Amen!

Prophetic Word

Separate yourself from the world unto Me, for you are the Righteous.

I am your God, Father to all - but the Righteous are the true inheritors of their inheritance in Jesus Christ. Speaketh Me, speaketh words of righteousness, so says the Lord your God, Father to all.

Speaketh, sing, rejoice - for Christ is coming, He is near!

Missiles of fire to be launched upon this earth, fire to cleanse the earth from the unrighteous.

I cleanse, I purge, My wrath is righteous upon all – for those who abide in My law I have salvation, for those who refuse I have predestined death eternal.

Rejoice – for Christ is coming...He is near.

Rejoice for the day of reckoning are here, the day for your return to Me are at hand. That is My order and will – manifested in you, the righteous!

Rejoice – for the day of reckoning is here, it is at hand! Conform to the righteousness of Jesus Christ.

For His righteousness is My righteousness!

Save yourselves in Christ, conform to My Truth. Rejoice!

Remain diligent at the Altar, remain steadfast at the Altar, remain tethered to Me through Christ, your God of all. Speaketh Words of Wisdom unto those in darkness. For thou who knoweth not what they do, walk in blindness, led astray by Satan,

but you have received the anointing and know the difference between error and truth. Remain steadfast, remain diligent, so sayeth the God, your Father.

Speaketh no evil, do righteousness.

Remain at the Altar for your salvation is at hand. God's time-line is not the time-line of the world, but is according to His Will and His Plan.

The time of Righteousness is the time-line of the Week of Righteousness, nearing its completion.

For the time is at hand for you to return to Me, so sayeth the Lord your God. Righteousness unto all those who walk in obedience to My Word and Will.

For I have received you before you were born, sent to the place of unrighteousness for your reforming unto righteousness.

So praise God,

Lord of all those who abide in the Light. Saved, you are in Christ – My Holy Son...

Send to this world for your sin. Buying you free from condemnation, releasing you from the bondage placed upon your forefathers ... because of sin and disobedience.

Speaketh Words of Wisdom – wise people of Mine, for you have been chosen by Me unto righteousness. Saved by the Light that is in Me.

I have written My Word within your mind and hearts.

You are saved through Christ, Almighty Father to all the Righteous ones. Saved you are by My Word.

You are righteous – imputed upon you by me,

because of your faith and obedience to Me and My Word. Praise Me in song and deed.

Pray, for your salvation is near and at hand. Glorify God through your deeds of righteousness.

For in Me you are righteous, you are just, you are perfect, you are holy, you are Mine! So sayeth the Lord your God.

Give Satan no heed, spoiler of faith is he, unjust is he...robber of faith – speaketh Words of Righteousness -

Words of faith – so sayeth the Lord your God.

Praise Me, sing unto Me in the Spirit o' righteous ones. For your praise is My pleasure.

Your praise is My Life, given unto you by My power set in you through Christ. Save yourself in Christ. Remain at His Altar. Pray, Pray, Prophesy.

Speaketh My Word unto everyone,

remain not silent but speaketh Words of Wisdom, Words of Mystery. I will inspire you to speaketh the right words unto every man, Words of Wisdom – believeth in Me, I am at your side always, now and forever. Remain tethered to Me through Christ, heed not the words of Satan, his words of unrighteousness – for he is there to spoil your faith, rob you from faith - given a chance. This is the testing of your faith -

remain tethered to Me, for holy, holy, holy are you through Me.

Return to Me, soon you will… in all of Life and Light. Remain righteous – adorn the doctrine of Christ!

For the cloak of righteousness are yours to wear to all occasions now and forever. Remain tethered to Me, so sayeth the Lord your God… the God.

Remain in praise, remain in song, remain in prayer. So speaketh the Lord your God.

Remaining in Me is for Life, separated from Me is unto death. So speaketh to God, your Lord, your Father of all.

Inspired by the Holy Ghost My Words of Wisdom are brought to you, so focus on Me and My Life is yours for now and forever. My promises are complete, My promises are unbroken, everlasting,

for I am just and righteous, so says God the Spirit of all. Live your life in the fullness of Christ for He is your Saviour, brother to all righteous ones! Praise Him, glorify Him in word and deed so sayeth God, Father of all those given life by Me. Cloaked by righteousness you reflect My Image - pride and joy of God your Father.

Glorify Me! Glorify Me! Reflect Me, you are My firstborn. Rejoice!

Rejoice, your return are at hand… be prepared, stay prepared,

I am like a thief in the night, I come without warning…

but you are warned by Me of My coming - unawares you are not. Praise Me! Praise Me! Rejoice in Me, rejoice in Me! So sayeth the Lord the God, Father of all.

Remain diligent! Remain prepared!

Prophetic Word

Praise God to all nations and Righteous ones! Listen to My Voice o' righteous!

For I speaketh unto you o' blessed ones!

Remain diligent at the Altar, for the time has come for My return unto this world, harvesting those who bear My fruit, reflecting My Face through diligence and consistency at the Altar. Praise God o' Righteous ones – for I am here at the door awaiting the time of entrance.

Praise God o' Righteous ones, for I love them who loveth Me through My Son!

Blessed is he who knoweth Me.

Blessed is he who walks after the Spirit.

The time has come o' world to repent of thy evil ways, harken to My Voice, listen to My Words, repent and return unto Me!

So sayeth the Lord your God, creator of all things and nations!

Harken to My Word, to My Will, listen to My Voice! Abide within the Law I have set in My Son Christ Jesus, for redemption comes through this Law set in Him, none other! Walk in Covenant with Me, synchronize your steps with that of the Holy Spirit, Blessed is he who abides in Me – for ever and ever!

I calleth, you answereth and so you are saved through Christ Jesus!

Harken to My Voice o' blessed ones – for thy are My chosen. Remain at the Altar, for the time is near at hand I speaketh words of Mercy unto those who listen to My Voice, I remain at your side forever and ever.

Remain diligent, remain steadfast, remain tethered to Me through Christ Jesus, your Saviour and Redeemer. Listen not to the voice of Satan – for he rules through fear, asserting himself as the blessed but cursed by Me unto death eternal.

Remain strong. Remain focused, for the time is near. Be obedient unto My Word of Life.

Save yourself through Christ.

Your sovereignty is for choice of faith, I do not intervene. Thou showeth love unto Me through obedience in faith, thus I love thee the same.

Praise God o' Righteous ones! Praise God o' children of Light. For blessed are they who harken to My Voice, so sayeth the Lord your God – creator of all.

Blessed are he who knoweth the signs of the time of return – for so shall they know of My coming.

Be brave o' Blessed ones. Remain steadfast, for you are My chosen ones in whom I am well pleased.

Reflecting My Son Christ Jesus.

Glory unto all those who abide in Me, so sayeth the Lord – God of all.

Blessed is he who knoweth the signs of the times, for so they are forewarned to return to Me with haste and diligence, seeking My pleasure in all things. Revealed unto you are My Words of Mercy, to remain at the Altar until the time of My coming which is soon. Blessed are they whom harken to these words of Mine - for they will inherit the true royal inheritance as co-inheritors with Christ Jesus.

Blessed are they who dispute not My Words for being a lie, saved are you who repent through Christ Jesus, dying unto the self, forsaking all else, no idols within, clear skies above as heaven moves nearer to earth.

My Will is My Testament, given unto all those who listen and harken to the Words I speak.

Forsake not the Covenant of Grace, but remain steadfast -for all else is of death and you are resurrected unto Life in Christ. Praise God o' Righteous ones, for blessed is he who listens to My Words of Mercy – blessed is he who repent, remain tethered to Me, remain steadfast o' Righteous ones.

For the world shall mourn its ignorance and arrogance, resisting Me and tempting Me unto wrath and anger, forsaking the bond I have made with Abraham for all eternity to come. Forsaking Me is unto death, evil ways have no place in My House, the path of righteousness is unto Life.

Forsaking Me shall bring death to those who resist the Covenant of God – for arrogance brings eternal death and separation from Me.

Harken to My Voice o' Righteous ones, for as I say this to you in this day so it shall be -

My wrath shall be poured out upon those who rejected My Covenant forsaking Me unto their own peril, death shall be their friend eternally.

So says God your Father, to all from above and beyond.

Harken to My Voice, I am tempted by those who resist My Grace, provoked by those who reject the Covenant. Blaspheme not the Lord o' Righteous – for the perilous way of those who reject is death eternal.

Lift up your eyes to heaven, My Way is your way, life eternal in My Bosom so sayeth God your Father.

Reject not My hand of friendship and love, for the reward is death eternal.

Unto those whom resist, I say this, deliverance is not by man but through Christ,

repent or experience My wrath that will be poured out upon the land soon.

I harken not to the voice of man, I listen not to his whispers of mercy that reflect the knowledge of death – but rather you should listen to Me as I speak these words of Mercy unto you - for if you refuse, the punishment shall be death eternal in the fire of hell's gate.

Amen!

Conclusion

In the beginning, God created Adam and Eve in the garden of Eden, in His Presence. Because of their disobedience to God, He cast them out of his Presence. From that day people have been living out of the Presence of God. Jesus is coming for his church, it's time for God's people to come back in his Presence..

Light and Darkness do not mix, you either walk in the Light or the Darkness, there is no inbetween. Light=Jesus, Darkness=Satan. John 8:12 Nkjv; The spake Jesus unto them,saying, I Am the Light of the world: he that followeth me shall not walk in Darkness, but shall have the Light of life.

1 John 1:5-7 Nkjv; This then is the message which we have heard of Him, and declare unto you, that God is Light, and in Him is no Darkness at all.

V6: If we say that we have fellowship with Him, and walk in Darkness, we lie, and do not the truth: V7:But If walk in the Light as He is in the Light, we have fellowship one with another, and the blood of Jesus Christ His son cleanses us from all sin.

Romans 13:12

12 The night is far spent, the day is at hand: let us therefore cast off the works of Darkness, and let us put on the armor of Light.

John 3:19:21

19 And this is the condemnation, that Light has come into the world, men loved Darkness rather than Light, because their deeds were evil.

20 For every one that doeth evil hateth the Light, neither cometh to the Light, lest his deeds should be reproved.

21 But he that doeth truth cometh to the Light, that his deeds may be made manifest that they be wrought in God.

Those who are hearing Jesus will walk in the Light daily. The point is everyone has ears to hear and will have free will to decide how to walk those who are after the things of the world will suffer one day if they don't surrender to JESUS CHRIST. Rebellious hearts can only be changed by the Holy Spirit. All people are created in God's image and no life is beyond God's reach if people would receive His way for Salvation. It is time for the Church to Awake from its Slumber before it's too late. The true Shepherd Jesus is coming for His sheep you are my flock the flock of my pasture you are men and I am your God says the Lord . God the Lord will be Israel's Shepard. Jesus only not the doctrines of men.

Revelations 22

12 And behold, I come quickly, and my reward is with me, to give every man according as his works shall be.

13 I am Alpha and Omega, the beginning and the end, the first and the last.

14 Blessed are they that do his commandments, that they may have right to the tree of life, and may enter in through the gate to the city.

15 For without are dogs, and sorcerers, and woremongers, and murderers, and idolaters, and whosoever loveth and maketh a lie.

16 I Jesus have sent mine angel to testify unto you these things in the churches. I Am the root and offspring of David, and the bright and morning star.

17 And the Spirit and the bride say, Come. And let him that heareth say, come. And let him that is a thirst come. And whosoever will, let him take the water of life freely.

18 For I testify unto every man that heareth the words of the prophecy of this book, If any man shall add unto these things, God shall add unto him the plagues that are written in this book:

19 And if any man shall take away from the words of the book of this prophecy, God shall take away his part out of the book of life, and out of the holy city, and from the things which are written in this book.

20 He who testifieth these things saith, Surely I come quickly. Amen. Even so, come, Lord Jesus.

21 The grace of our Lord Jesus Christ be with you all. Amen.

People of the WORLD it is time for us to Awake from our Slumber. For the King of Kings and Lord of LORDS is returning for His bride His CHURCH. We are responsible for our own Salvation that's why we were given freewill. On the day of the JUDGMENT of Christ Jesus we will answer for ourselves to be ready people of GOD be ready for JESUS.

www.ingramcontent.com/pod-product-compliance
Lightning Source LLC
Chambersburg PA
CBHW071410181224
19222CB00029B/923